Reflections
from the
Manse Window

by

Rev. Ian W. F. Hamilton

A collection of short stories many of which were originally published
in 'The People's Friend' or broadcast on Grampian Television

With every blessing

Ian Hamilton .

First published September 1992
© Ian W. F. Hamilton 1992
ISBN 1 870151 03 8

Printed and Published by
MORAVIAN PRESS LTD.
31 SOUTH STREET ELGIN MORAY IV30 1LA
1992

To Margaret, David, Gillian and Jennifer
for their constant and unfailing love and understanding
from behind the manse window.

REV. IAN W. F. HAMILTON, B.D., L.TH., A.L.C.M., A.V.C.M.

Employed initially in banking, the Rev. Ian William Finlay Hamilton was ordained to the Ministry of the Church of Scotland in October 1978, when he was inducted into Alloa North Parish Church, his first charge. In October 1986 he was called to be Minister at Nairn Old Parish Church, one of the largest charges in the north of Scotland.

Ian Hamilton's main interest, outside his family, is music. He was for some years Organist and Choirmaster in his home congregation, the former charge of Gordon Park, Glasgow, and he holds London College diplomas in pianoforte.

Married to Margaret in 1971, the Hamiltons have three children, David who is thirteen, and twins Gillian and Jennifer aged ten.

Ian is a regular contributor to Grampian Television's "Reflections" programme and also to the popular weekly magazine, "The People's Friend." Additionally he has in recent years participated in regular summer pulpit exchanges to the Wyckoff Reformed Church in New Jersey, USA.

FOREWORD

by

Rev. Dr. James Martin

M.A., B.D., D.D.

I am delighted to have the honour of writing a short Foreword to this, Ian Hamilton's first book. My delight is made all the greater by virtue of the fact that I am in no doubt that there will be many people who will find "Reflections from the Manse Window" not only an enjoyable read but also a source of real help and inspiration for the business of daily living.

Through the media of "The People's Friend" and Grampian Television many readers will already have met Ian Hamilton and a good number of the stories contained in this book. Here, in a different environment, they will encounter again the author's keen observation of human life and his ability to extract lessons from ordinary and not so ordinary happenings.

It is good that this publication will bring Ian Hamilton and his 'taken from life' anecdotes to an even wider public; and I am pleased to commend it to that public. This is a book for everybody; and everybody is sure to find something for himself or herself in it.

JAMES MARTIN

ACKNOWLEDGEMENTS

The greater part of this book is based on articles which were written for and have been published in 'The Peoples Friend' magazine.

The four 'Reflections' series were originally presented by the author on Grampian Television.

Grateful thanks is expressed to D. C. THOMSON & CO. LTD., and to GRAMPIAN TELEVISION P.L.C. for permitting these to be re-used in written form, and to D. C. THOMSON & CO. LTD. for allowing the illustrations on pages 15, 37, 39, 42, 44 and 49 to be reproduced.

Illustrations on pages 33, 35, 55 and 56 are by David Hamilton.

Cover illustration by Evelyn Pottie, Broombank, Loch Flemington.

CONTENTS

'Reflections from the Manse Window'

by

Rev. Ian W. F. Hamilton

A Symbol of Welcome

WE spent a delightful few days recently at Crieff Hydro Hotel in beautiful Perthshire. Crieff, as many of you will know is a picturesque spot and it's our custom to go there around this time of year and meet up with other ministers and their families. Many friendships between manse families have been forged there over the years and it's great to renew them on the occasion of these annual get-togethers.

There are two morning rituals that have become regular features of our Hydro breaks — first of all, following breakfast, morning prayers in the magnificent drawing room complete with pipe organ! While it's always a privilege to lead the hotel guests in this short act of worship — as ministers who are staying in the Hydro are invited to do — I must say I normally find myself presiding at the organ console leading the singing! And I thoroughly enjoy the change of role — even just for a few short days.

Following prayers, the second ritual is to then head down into Crieff for morning coffee — as if we hadn't had our fill at breakfast time! On our last visit to the town we came across a new coffee shop which had just opened for business. What particularly attracted our attention and persuaded us that we should go in was a sign stuck on to the inside glass panel in the front door. No, it wasn't 'welcome' (although we were!) nor was it 'open' (as indeed it was) nor was it 'no prams or pushchairs' (we're all past that stage anyway!) Rather the sign took the form of a fish — it was the outline of a fish, which meant that the coffee shop was owned and run by a Christian family. And in order to indicate this they displayed this special and ancient symbol on their entrance door.

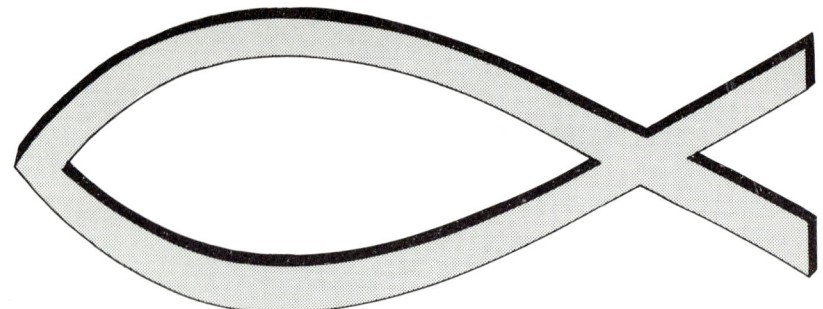

The sign in fact goes back to New Testament times, to the days of the early church when the people of the new movement had to meet in secret. So really, the sign of the fish was a secret sign and the folks of the faith used it to point to the place where they were going to meet. The early Christians knew what the sign meant and they followed it and so came together to praise and worship Jesus.

The symbol of the fish had been adopted because Jesus himself had used the metaphor when he invited the two sets of brothers, Simon and Andrew and James and John down by the lakeside to follow him and become "fishers of men". The people whom they in turn brought to Jesus had been 'caught' like fish in a net!

Happily in our day and age Christian people don't need to meet in secret when they come together to praise and worship God, and indeed at this time when walls and barriers are coming down increasingly in other lands we give thanks to God for the new found freedom Christian people world-wide can now enjoy.

More and more, people, like us, are now able to openly and joyfully express their faith, worship their God and sing his praises! Perhaps they do so in the words of the ever-popular chorus:

"I will make you fishers of men,
Fishers of men, fishers of men.
I will make you fishers of men
If you follow me!"

Oh — incidentally, the friendly Christian welcome we got in the new coffee shop at Crieff was a delight . . . . as was the coffee!

"Wide, wide as the ocean!"

DO any of you remember from your Sunday School days the popular children's chorus, "Wide, wide as the ocean, high as the heavens above, deep, deep as the deep blue sea is my Saviour's love!" What a super chorus it was — and indeed IS! It's still tremendously popular, and not only with the boys and girls!

In fact, not so very long ago the Church of Scotland organised a very special evening in Glasgow for those in the Kirk who, over the years, had assisted with the work of Summer Mission (or Seaside Mission as it was once called). It took place in the City Hall and there were hundreds present, including the then Moderator of the General Assembly, who himself had been part and parcel of Seaside Mission in former days.

The crowd were enthusiastic to say the least and a choir of over a hundred was specially formed to lead the singing, which I had the pleasure of accompanying on the City Hall concert grand piano — what a thrill! The singing was marvellous — they literally raised the roof, and on that evening anyway the famous Hampden roar was even put into second place! All the well-loved choruses were on the programme, choruses and songs that have featured over the years at so many venues around the Scottish coast. And yes, you've guessed — right at the very top of the programme was "Wide, wide as the ocean!" Over and over again they sang it with great gusto and at the very tops of their voices!

Of course the love of Jesus Christ IS something to sing about — and its something to sing about whatever the circumstances, whatever the situation.

I'm reminded of the story of the young minister with a young family who, some years ago had just tragically lost his dear wife. He decided to take his family — following their tragedy — to visit some relatives who lived in the U.S.A., and so they set sail. One cool afternoon mid-Atlantic when the minister and his children were standing at the ship's rail looking out to sea, his young daughter suddenly asked her dad the question, "Tell me daddy, how great is God's love?" Her father replied, "Well my dear, if you look out here on the port side of the ship as far as your eye can see, and then if you look to the starboard side as far as your eye can see . . . and then if you look high above you into the clear blue sky and deep down to the bottom of this great ocean, as far as you could possibly go

4

. . . *that's* how great God's love is!" the girl's father reassured her. "Isn't it funny," the wee girl added, "that we're right in the middle of it!"

I'm sure this lovely story is a kind of parable of what the great St Paul had in mind when he spoke and wrote about the 'breadth, length, height and depth of the love of Christ'. This love, this love "so amazing, so divine" as the hymn-writer referred to it — wide as the ocean, high as the heavens above, deep, deep as the deep blue sea, as the popular chorus refers to it, is OUR SAVIOUR'S LOVE!

And be assured, it is active in our world yesterday, today and forever . . . and as the wee girl remarked . . . WE'RE RIGHT IN THE MIDDLE OF IT!

"Emergency Religion!"

I F ever there were to be such a thing as the "Hymn Charts" — as opposed to the "Pop Charts" — I'm pretty sure that the well-loved hymn "What a friend we have in Jesus" would always be right there at the very TOP of the charts!

Occasionally here in Nairn Old we hold "YOUR FAVOURITE HYMN" praise services where the congregation choose what hymns will be sung by posting their favourites into our Hymn Postbox during the weeks leading up to the special service. "What a friend we have in Jesus" ALWAYS receives an enormous number of votes — and so inevitably it is included!

Of course it's a hymn about PRAYER - perhaps you'll remember these familiar lines:

"O what peace we often forfeit
O what needless pain we bear,
All because we do not carry
Everything to God in *prayer*."

Prayer is so *vital* to the Christian way of life — in fact it has been described as the lifeline of communication between each one of us and our God. It's a natural, human habit, and when I meet annually with those wishing to become members of the church, invariably I begin the "prayer" session by asking those present if there is any one of them who *hasn't* prayed at some time in the past. Happily I have never yet met anyone who *hadn't* prayed at some point during the course of their lives!

Many have admitted however that they tended only to pray in the emergencies of life. "You're not alone!" I forever assure them — countless people connect prayer only with times of calamity and of crisis, personal or national — it's then and only then that prayer for so many comes into play.

"EMERGENCY RELIGION" it's sometimes called — and to to illustrate it I usually tell a story I once heard . . . . of a man who, while out in the country one day found himself in the middle of a large field. In the far corner he suddenly saw a large bull — a large angry-looking bull! — and to make matters worse, the man was wearing a bright red shirt! What was he to do? There was no point in running, the field was so vast — and the bull was already charging towards him! He could always pray he thought, but then he had never done much praying — what would he say? And then suddenly the inspiration he was so desperately looking for came to him. He raised his eyes to the heavens and uttered the only prayer he had ever known: "For what I am about to receive, may the Lord make me truly thankful!"

For so many alas, it's only when they are up against it or when they are in a situation of illness, or danger, or worry or anxiety that they would ever think of "taking it to the Lord in prayer" as the popular hymn suggests. It is inevitable of course that for all of us our prayers will be more intense at some times than at others — and it's RIGHT that we should pray in the emergencies of life — GOD WANTS TO HEAR THESE PRAYERS, BE SURE!

But prayer, for all of us, should be a regular, constant thing, and as I ever encourage my church members, new and not so new(!) come rain, come shine, always take time to PRAY. As Paul the apostle said long ago: "In *everything* by prayer and supplication, with thanksgiving let your requests be made known to God."

SOME "REFLECTIONS" . . . .

MONDAY

(Cue Ian at piano . . . . 30 seconds of 'Morning has Broken')

> "Morning has broken, like the first morning,
> Blackbird has spoken, like the first bird.
> Praise for them singing, praise for the morning,
> Praise for them springing fresh from the world."

This is the second morning of a new year which has broken — and God willing another 363 have still to break! And hand in hand with every new morning that breaks (with all its blessings) there goes surely this note of praise, of thanks — for the singing of the birds — for the new morning itself.

And yes, as the song has it, it was God who gave us that very first new morning — and all the new mornings ever since!

There's a lovely "morning" story at the end of St John's gospel in the Bible when Jesus, now risen, showed himself to his disciples on the beach and shared breakfast with them — and for them that was a special morning indeed! When they realised who the stranger on the shore really was they were ecstatic!

In this new year ahead begin each God-given day in the company of Jesus, and for you too every new morning will be special!

A very good morning to you!

(Ian plays a further 20 seconds of "Morning has Broken".)

TUESDAY

(Cue Ian at piano . . . . 25 seconds of "I have Confidence in Me.")

Do you recognise these few opening bars? They're from the song, "I have confidence in me" from the ever-popular "Sound of Music". You MUST have seen the film — at least five times!

Julie Andrews sings it at the point where she has just been rejected as the novice would-be Sister Maria. Having to be content as Frauline Maria she now contemplates (and not without a little fear and trepidation) her new role in life as governess to the seven Von Trapp children. And as she does she sings these words — "What will the day be like, I wonder? What will the future be, I wonder?" All of us would echo Frauline Maria's words — and especially at the outset of a new year.

But as the song progresses Maria concludes that she has confidence .
. . . confidence in sunshine, and in rain and in the fact that spring will come
again!

Another way in which to express "confidence" is "sure and certain hope"
— and what Maria is really saying is that she HAS confidence (or hope)
in the GIVER of all these things, namely GOD.

The words of a hymn we sing in Church say something very similar —
"MY HOPE (CONFIDENCE) IS BUILT ON NOTHING LESS THAN
JESUS' BLOOD AND RIGHTEOUSNESS."

A very good morning to you!

(Ian plays a further 14 seconds of "I have Confidence in Me.")

WEDNESDAY

(Cue Ian at piano . . . . 17 seconds of "Memories of the Way We Were.")

"Memories of the way we were" — the film theme song! New Year is
undoubtedly a time for memories — they come flooding back to us around
now, of things and of days that were. And yes, often amid the confusion
of today perhaps we even yearn to be the way we were! But things ARE
as they ARE and we must live for the moment!

The Children of Israel wandering in the wilderness and desperately short
of food and water once complained to Moses that he should have left them
the way they were. "We would have been better off back in Egypt, at least
we had food and water there" they protested.

But God soon came to their rescue, and manna from heaven and water
out of the rock were duly provided!

Thankful for our memories of the way we were we must live for the
moment and face the future with faith. God will provide for you, and for
me too, come what may! Just you wait and see!

A very good morning to you!

(Ian plays a further 34 seconds of "Memories").

THURSDAY

(Cue Ian at piano . . . . 20 seconds of "It's the Good Life!")

Do you recognise that one? . . . . a Sinatra evergreen! . . . . "It's the Good
Life!"

And do you realise that there are only around 350 shopping days left
till Christmas? None the less, I expect, like me, you're glad to see the mad
seasonal scramble over for another year!

During these post-Christmas weeks many go through the annual ritual
of Christmas Swapping, as the High Street stores call it. The children got
dad's collar size wrong — his 15 inch shirt must be exchanged for a 15½

if he's going to get any use out of his gift. But dad got his wife's measurements wrong too, and so she has to swap here size 10 jumper for a size 18 . . . . or whatever (I never was an authority on ladies' sizes!)

Christmas swapping! The shops have come to accept it as a normal part of the Christmas season.

But you know there are some gifts which are simply impossible to exchange — the gift of LIFE for example. It IS a good life, and although none of us were responsible for our own coming into existence, few of us I expect would have chosen NOT to have been given this particular gift! Oh maybe some might have chosen a different heritage or a different station in life, had that been possible, but life comes AS IT IS!

And to make the most of the life that's been given to us — AS IT IS — and AS WE ARE — is to respond to God, the giver of ALL life, in the highest way.

We simply couldn't EXCHANGE life for anything! Nor should we want to!

Thanks be to God for "THE GOOD LIFE" — Make the most of it in the day, and in the YEAR ahead!

(Ian plays a further 25 seconds of "It's the Good Life!")

FRIDAY

(Cue Ian at piano . . . . 23 seconds of "Many a New Day.")

"Many a new day will please my eye, many a new love will find me!" — from "Oklahoma". There are many new days ahead of us during the new year just begun. I suppose the important thing is how we will USE them — how we will fill them.

To use our days, which God gives us, to the full is what is surely important. It was Thomas a Kempis who in the 15th century wrote: "Would to God that we might spend a single day really well!" God I'm sure wants us to spend *every* day really well — and to the full! And God, in Jesus Christ, gives us the perfect pattern as to how we should so do.

Read for yourself the opening chapters of St Mark's gospel in the Bible, and there you will find a catalogue of vivid pictures of a typical packed-full day in the life of Jesus. One duty just piled on top of another. People sick of mind and of body came clamouring after him, and often into the night, and never was any one of them sent away unhelped.

Jesus filled HIS days helping and serving others . . . . now there's a way of using to the full the many new days God will give you in the new year ahead!

HAVE A NICE NEW DAY!

(Ian plays a further 25 seconds of "Many a New Day.")

"Art Thou Troubled?"

A particular class in a school to which I was once Chaplain were engrossed in a story entitled, "John's Grumpy Granny". I asked the boys and girls about the story and of course they were only too happy to elucidate!

Apparently everything had been tried in order to make the old woman happy again — but to no avail. The family were so desperate to find a cure for her grumpiness that even the village doctor had been called in. All sorts of wonderful potions and magic medicines were prescribed — but again, to no avail. Suddenly it occurred to John, her young grandson, that if he went to visit his granny and greet her with a smile on his face and with a note of cheerfulness in his voice, it might just do the trick . . . . and it did! (And they all lived happily ever after!)

I reminded the children of a parallel story — albeit an ancient one, which is to be found in the Bible. The parallel story concerns, not a granny, but a king who lived in Old Testament times — a moody, unhappy king whose name was Saul. His bleak, black moods were coming upon him all too frequently, and nothing had been found so far to bring him out of his moods. Eventually one of the palace servants suggested that what he needed was *music* to calm him down and to make him forget all his troubles. The young man who administered the music was a certain shepherd lad called David — and the rest, as they say, is history.

Recently one of my parishoners very suddenly lost his dear life's partner, and he was heart broken — especially so since Bob himself had previously been at death's door on several occasions.

Art thou troubled

Words by W. G. ROTHERY
Larghetto

Music by HANDEL
(From " Rondelinda ")

Art . . thou trou bled?   Mu - sic   will calm thee,

10

Amidst his sorrow he was thinking back no doubt to the many times when his dear wife had been such a tremendous strength and support to him in every way during his own health crises — and he was 'taking it badly' to say the least. In the days and weeks immediately following Mary's death, Bob was swamped with kindness and support from family, from neighbours, from his doctor, and, I am happy to say, from the Kirk.

Bob isn't strictly speaking a member of the Parish Kirk, although he has many friends who are members. But he lives within the bounds of the parish and accordingly he comes under the parish umbrella in terms of pastoral care — which was readily offered. Besides, he and his late wife often supported the various functions in the Parish Church — and especially those of a *musical* nature.

In the course of conversation during a post-funeral visit Bob happened to mention a particularly successful 'Festival of Praise' we had put on a year or so previously in the Church. He and Mary had been there and they had enjoyed it immensely. "I happen to have a video of that occasion at home in the manse Bob — would you like to have a look at it sometime?" I willingly offered. He readily took up my offer and a week or so later Bob came back to the manse door to return the tape.

I detected immediately a marked change in him — the sparkle was back in his eye, and despite his sad loss which he was still trying to come to terms with, his attitude appeared decidedly more positive. "That's the best medicine anyone could have given me Mr Hamilton! I found more comfort in that tape than I have been able to find anywhere else in these last few weeks, despite the best intentions of all the good folks rallying around me." A copy of the 'Festival' tape has recently been handed in to Bob's home.

"Art thou troubled — music will calm thee."

Just as there are ministries of word and of sacrament, so too are there ministries of friendship, of comfort, of companionship, of laughter and of MUSIC . . . . and be sure, God can use every one of them!

Take your stand!

PART of our family holiday this year was spent on the beautiful sun-drenched island of Jersey in the Channel Islands.

What a lovely and interesting island — lovely in terms of the picturesque bays all around its shores, and interesting in terms of the memorabilia from the German Occupation during the last war.

David, our son, was particularly interested to visit the many German bunkers still there on the island largely undisturbed since the war years. When Hitler gave his orders in October 1941 to turn the British Channel Islands into "impregnable fortresses", thousands of slave workers were imported from Europe to construct concrete fortifications such as the coastal bunkers and the tunnels of the famous Underground Hospital.

The experience of visiting such venues was, for both David and dad, chilling to say the least and made us realise in a very real way some of the trials and tribulations of the war years, which neither of us of course have lived through.

In the course of our Jersey holiday we took a day trip to Brittany in France. We travelled by hydrofoil and arrived at the historic walled city of St Malo, whereupon we were taken on a bus tour of some of the small coastal towns of North Brittany — and in particular to a lovely wee place called Saint Lumière.

The houses there were "just out of this world" as they say! The policy in France — in that area anyway — is not to buy a house as such, but to purchase a piece of land and have your home built on it to your own design and specification — and they were really magnificent, *except one* — you had to see it to believe it!

Within the bounds of this very beautiful and very 'posh' estate there stood (just and no more!) a rickety old shack! It had been built, physically, by a woman of over eighty years of age — she used anything at all she could find — driftwood from the beach — odd pieces of corrugated iron she had come across — and she bought the odd bag of cement! There were bricks everywhere and anywhere — it was the proverbial eyesore!

Naturally the authorities weren't too pleased, especially as they tend to be rather more strict with that kind of thing over there, but the old woman rebelled against the authorities — relentlessly! She took her stand — and she got away with it! Now whether she was right or wrong in so doing you can judge for yourself — I'm not going to say! Nevertheless she took her stand, and her wee house is still standing there in Saint Lumiere . . . at least it was about nine weeks ago!

Someone once said: "Stand for something or you'll fall for anything!" And indeed all of us take our various stands relating to all sorts of issues in life. It may be in the field of politics — we stand for the aims and policies of this party or of that one. We may stand for the right to work or for the freedom to speak. We all, I'm sure, stand for truth and for peace and for justice for all men and women. We stand firm for all sorts of noble and excellent causes.

It's important that we so do and it is important further that we make what we stand for clear to others — like the wee lady of Saint Lumière — her shack was situated right at the kerbside, unlike the other houses which were set well back. Her's was so placed that all could *see* the stand she was taking — they couldn't miss it!

It is particularly important for the people of God to make clear to others what they stand for, and indeed what the Church of which they are part stands for. Things like Christian fellowship, friendship, faith, joy and surely, love.

And all of these can be summed up compendiously and completely in one word — in one name. In the words of the well-loved hymn: "Stand up, stand up for JESUS!" Because if you stand for him — *and are seen to stand for him* — you won't fall for anything, or for anyone!

The joy in finding

FOLLOWING a recent story of mine which was published in the "Friend" a regular reader in the south of England contacted Nairn Old Parish Church office. She had lost track of one of her cousins many years previously, and the only information she had about her long lost relative was that she lived somewhere in the Nairn area. It had been so long since they had been in contact that the only name which the lady could give to my secretary when she phoned was her cousin's maiden name. Anne searched the church and parish records relentlessly, but alas, to no avail.

"All is not lost however" thought Anne, "I'll ask Jack — he's sure to know something about this lady!" Jack Ferries is our Church Officer at Nairn Old, and being a senior citizen born and bred in the area he's a goldmine of information on the townsfolk, and especially on those who have lived in and around Nairn over the years. And yes, Jack *did* know of the lady in question and very soon thereafter — in a matter of days — the long lost cousins were re-united!

A few weeks later I received a lovely letter from Mrs McDonald thanking all of us for bringing the reunion about. She kindly wrote as follows: "I read your recent story in the "People's Friend" which I found very enjoyable, but little did I think at the time that I would also find something — or *someone* — through your story! Jean and I have now found each other again after forty years!"

The Bible contains several stories, or parables as they are called, that could well be entitled "Lost and Found" stories. Jesus himself told many of these picture stories, and they are recorded for us in the gospels. In one particular chapter of St Luke's gospel Jesus tells us of a shepherd who lost one of his sheep — of a woman who lost one of her coins — and of a father who lost one of his two sons. And as our Lord's picture stories unfold, what is so apparent is the care that is taken to FIND the thing (or the person) that is lost, and also the joy that is experienced when it is found again.

When the lost sheep is returned safely to the fold, and when the shepherd shouts out joyously at the top of his voice, Jesus says, "That's what God is like!" When the woman's coin is found again, and when she calls all her friends and neighbours together for a celebration, Jesus says, "That's what God is like!" When the wayward son, realising his folly, trudges homeward once more, and when his forgiving father runs out to welcome him with open arms, Jesus says, "That's what God is like!" The whole point in Jesus telling these picture stories was in order that those to whom he spoke could understand Almighty God as a loving, caring and forgiving Father.

When the lost is found again, the experience for those concerned is always one of ecstatic joy. We can well understand the happiness shared by these two cousins who had lost each other for over forty years! And perhaps we can understand also the happiness experienced by God, our heavenly and forgiving Father, when we too become re-united with him! From time to time each one of us strays off in our own foolish ways, and when we do this we become "lost" to God — sometimes over many years.

We can be assured however through these picture stories Jesus told, that when we are "found" again, the experience of our Father in heaven is one of ecstatic joy — a Father who is always seeking us out, and who on finding us, treats us as if we had never been away!

We will remember them

DURING my summer holiday to Jersey in the Channel islands, I was delighted to see that the "Friend" was just as available there as it is on the mainland — and, let me add, it's just as popular on the Island!

Of course when you mention Jersey these days you immediately think of the highly popular television series, 'Bergerac' — and one of the highlights of the holiday for our three children was to actually *meet* Jim Bergerac (the actor John Nettles) and to have their photograph taken with him sitting in that famous old car!

Bergerac (John Nettles) and Jennifer (Margaret and Gillian in background)

However long before the lovely island was invaded by the television moguls to film 'Bergerac' it suffered from a rather more irksome invasion. In July 1940 the German army occupied the Channel islands by force — in fact it was the only foothold the Nazis gained on British soil during the war years, and still today there are many living on these islands who have rather unpleasant memories, to say the least, of these bleak years they spent under seige — years of deprivation, of tyranny and of despair.

Today Jersey has several wartime reminders which serves as popular tourist attractions . . . the many bunkers for example around the rugged coastline, the German Army Headquarters at Strawberry Farm buried deep below ground level in the centre of the island, and not least the famous German Underground Hospital built by thousands of forced labourers working under the most atrocious conditions as they created tunnels over a mile in length out of solid rock. Sad days indeed.

During the five years of the occupation many people living in Jersey, but not born there, were deported from the island to German internment camps, and in the island's beautiful Howard Davis Park, visitors to Jersey today can see a memorial stone dedicated to the memory of those who were despatched from the island during the German occupation, and who did not survive the duration of the war. Also however, in a corner of this lovely park, visitors are able to visit a war cemetery — and to do so is a very poignant and humbling experience let me assure you. The cemetery was dedicated in November 1943 as a resting place for the bodies of members of the Allied Forces which had been recovered within the Bailiwick of Jersey during the terrible years of the Second World War. Stretching before their eyes visitors encounter rows and rows of simple wooden crosses — the majority of them, nameless. One among the many read as follows: "A NAVAL RATING, R.N. buried on 17th November, 1943" — and underneath there followed the stark yet comforting inscription, "KNOWN TO GOD". All who fought and died during the dark days of the two World Wars, and in all the wars since, were known to God — of that we can be sure, and we can be further sure that they were each LOVED by God.

But they were known to and loved by many of us too — by wives and sweethearts throughout the land, on continent and on island, and at this time of year particularly, with pride and with thanksgiving, WE REMEMBER THEM ALL.

In the familiar, yet priceless and irreplaceable words of the poet Laurence Binyon:

"AT THE GOING DOWN OF THE SUN AND IN THE MORNING . . . .
WE WILL REMEMBER THEM".

The War Cemetery in the Howard Davis Park, Jersey

17

"Little things mean a lot"

IN the words of the erstwhile popular song, "Little things mean a lot" and this is so true in so many areas of life. Very often it's not the big issues that break us as we live out our lives — somehow we're given the strength to cope with these. Rather it's the *small* things which gnaw away at us and the *petty* things that eat right into us which cause us endless anxiety.

In the opposite sense entirely however it's the small kindly things that are done *for* us and *to* us which can often mean so much. The quick phone call from a friend to ask how we are doing during an illness, or following the loss of a dear one, or in a time of family trouble or tension.

And then, what is true of small *things* is equally true I'm sure of small *places*. Perhaps when touring either at home or abroad during a holiday, it's the small and often rather trifling places that spring to mind when you come to think back on your holiday — small places or small towns which impressed you for one reason or another. LITTLE THINGS MEAN A LOT.

Christmas has been described in many ways, not least as the "greatest story ever told". Certainly no event in the annals of history has ever had such an infinite and inescapable impact on mankind. It was an event in eternity which will never be obliterated. It was indeed a cradle that rocked the world. God became human! The Lord became flesh and dwelt among us.

Yet at the time one must admit, the "great" earth-shattering event must have ranked of rather trifling significance to the majority of the people of the day. This seems particularly true when one looks at the *location* for the Almighty's momentous event. Bethlehem admittedly had had a long history — uniquely it was the city of David, and in former days the town had featured fairly prominently in Israel's history. But essentially Bethlehem was a *little* town, and by the time of the birth of Jesus, it was quite an unimportant little town. It was off the beaten track, and really, in truth it was a bit of a backwater. Many of the ordinary folks of the day perhaps hadn't even heard of it — and even if they had, it wasn't exactly the kind of place that they would have made a point of visiting . . . . and certainly it wasn't the kind of venue they would have imagined the Almighty to choose to launch "the greatest story ever told!"

None the less, the prophecy which 700 years earlier had graphically described this 'little town" came to pass: *"But you Bethlehem, small as you are to be among Judah's clans . . . . out of **you** shall come forth a governor of Israel."*

LITTLE THINGS MEAN A LOT . . . . especially where a certain little child is involved! As Isaiah the prophet had long since put it:

"Then a shoot shall grow from the stock of Jesse,
and a branch shall spring from his roots.
The spirit of the Lord shall rest upon him:
He shall judge the poor with justice
and defend the humble in the land with equity;
Then the wolf shall live with the sheep,
and the leopard lie down with the kid;
and the calf and the young lion shall
grow up together . . . . . .
AND A LITTLE CHILD SHALL LEAD THEM."

May the peace of the little child in the little town of Bethlehem be with you and yours this Christmastide and throughout the coming year.

O little town of Bethlehem,
How still we see thee lie!
Above thy deep and dreamless sleep
The silent stars go by;
Yet in thy dark streets shineth
The everlasting Light;
The hopes and fears of all the years
Are met in thee to-night.

19

Twin Symbols of Liberty

OUR pulpit exchange to the USA is just a memory now, but what a happy one! We established so many friendships among the good people of the New Jersey congregation to which I was attached and the hospitality they lavished on us was generous to say the least! Nothing was too much trouble for these folks to ensure that the Hamiltons felt truly at home among them — and we sure did!

They went out of their way to let us see all the sights and take us to as many places of interest as possible in the free time we had. And with New York City just a forty minute drive away via the famous George Washington Bridge there was plenty to see! Broadway, the Empire State Building, the twin towers of the World Trade Centre (higher than the Empire State Building), the United Nations Complex, the New York Seaport, Chinatown, the Rockefeller Centre and Central Park are just a few of the many Manhattan venues we were fortunate enough to visit.

However when anyone asks me, "What was the real highlight of your trip to the States?" I always single out our visit to the Statue of Liberty on Liberty Island in New York harbour. We had seen it in the movies, we had seen it in magazines, we had seen it on television, but NOW here was "Miss Liberty" in the flesh — in a manner of speaking! We were really THERE! — and not only were we gazing at her awsome magnificence from the outside, but we were actually climbing up the seemingly endless staircase (168 steps) deep inside her structure to reach her crown! And what a view from the top, across to Manhattan Island. David, my son, joined me in the climb to the crown and just to prove that we actually made it we took several photos of ourselves inside looking out through the windows of Miss Liberty's crown, and also photos of the magnificent view from the top!

The statue was originally gifted to the United States over a hundred years ago by France as memorial to American independence. It was designed by the French artist and sculptor Frederic Auguste Bartholdi, and the iron framework inside Miss Liberty to support the statue's copper skin was the work of his fellow countryman Gustave Eiffel — famous for a certain tower in Paris! The national monument has towered majestically there in New York harbour to greet visitors from all over the world, and a few years ago Miss Liberty's centenary was celebrated as only the Americans know how! In her right hand she holds high the torch as a beacon of light, and in her left hand she clutches the tablet which represents the statutes of the law.

As I took my last long look at her from the small boat which ferried us back over to Manhattan Island, I couldn't help thinking of that other symbol of liberty which once towered majestically on a hill called Calvary. Yes, the cross stood MAJESTICALLY because it bore on its beams a king — a king who claimed — long before the time of Miss Liberty — to be a light for all the world . . . . a king who, together with God his Father had long since given to mankind the holy statutes of *his* law, in the form of the ten commandments.

Perhaps it may all be summed up like this, I concluded:

The STATUE liberates the citizen,
The CROSS liberates the soul.

Yes, I'm sure my visit to Liberty Island was the highlight of my trip. It certainly gave me lots to think about.

Putting Nairn in the Picture

I T was quite an occasion when *"Scot 2"* arrived at Nairn Old Parish Church recently to record *"Songs of Praise"* for BBC Television!

"Scot 2" is one of the outside broadcast units belonging to BBC Scotland and it comprises of a fleet of four or five different vans and vehicles, each of which are necessary to enable the TV technicians to make this extremely popular programme. It's estimated that seven to eight million people tune in to *"Songs of Praise"* but very few of these viewers I imagine have little idea of the effort and months of preparation behind each programme.

What a happy occasion was Nairn's *"Songs of Praise!"* All the congregations in Nairn were invited to participate and in the end we had over 800 members from the local churches packed into the lovely Parish Church building for the final recording. The spirit of the occasion was good humoured to say the least — and the singing, which I had the privilege of conducting to the accompaniment of the Organ and Brass Ensemble, was glorious! The prayer and the blessing at the end of the programme was shared by the local Roman Catholic Priest and myself as Parish Minister, and five or six different denominations of Christ's Church all happily came together to sing — at the very tops of their voices — the praises of the God they all love and serve.

"Songs of Praise" is sold abroad now by the BBC, and so in due course the viewing audiences in Australia, New Zealand and Canada will have the pleasure of seeing in their own living rooms some super shots of the beautiful Moray Firth taken from the Nairn Old Parish Church tower!

As it happened, on the day on which our programme was being recorded, I was celebrating my birthday . . . and yes, you've guessed — they sang it! 800 voices to the accompaniment of a church organ and a brass band (the various parts for the instruments had been written out by the BBC Music Adviser!) together with the Series Editor up from London for the occasion conducting (with *my* baton!) they all sang *"Happy Birthday to you!"* I'm so relieved that the extra item was edited out of the final recording — but full marks to the boys from the BBC for making the occasion so special for yours truly!

Judging from the *countless* letters I received after the programme was transmitted it seems that the viewing public enjoyed it — and certainly the good folks of Nairn enjoyed making it. Every time we in the manse play

the video recording of the programme, memories come flooding back to us of the happy week we had when "Scot 2" was parked within the precincts of our kirk grounds.

But there's one particularly amusing incident I *must* share with you. David, my young son, was just desperate to have a look inside the main BBC vehicle, in which sat the programme director. The crew were most accommodating and a visit was duly arranged after school on one of the afternoons. David was thrilled to bits — as was Dad — surrounded by at least two million pounds worth of TV technology!

The source of amusement was to be found there in the Director's van. At the end of a facing row of several TV monitors there was a small glass panel about six inches square, on which was written; **"IN EMERGENCY BREAK GLASS"** *Behind* the glass there had been inserted a small 50p children's book entitled: **"TELEVISION — HOW IT WORKS!"** I must say it appealed to my sense of humour.

But more than that, it set me thinking. Isn't this perhaps what many people do with the Bible? Oh maybe they don't put it behind a glass panel exactly, but it's only in the emergencies of life that they ever think of opening it.

I'm reminded of the wee boy who lifted down a dusty Bible from the bookshelf and said, "Mummy, isn't this God's book?" "Oh yes John, you're right, it is God's book," replied his mother — to which John sharply responded — "Don't you think we should give him it back — we never use it?"

23

Learn . . . of me

ONE of the great privileges of contributing to this popular magazine must surely be the feedback which inevitably follows. Letters come to me regularly following particular stories I have had published — from all over the world! — and I am sure my ministerial colleagues who contribute to "The People's Friend" have found this to be their experience too.

Last week I received a letter from a "Friend" reader in New South Wales, Australia, expressing appreciation for a recent "Manse Window" article, and then Mrs Tookey went on to tell me about one of her grand-daughters. The incident had happened when the wee girl was about six years of age.

She had been going regularly to Sunday School for a couple of years or so and she had just arrived home one Sunday when who came to visit but Gran and Grandpa. "Hello my dear," said Gran, "have you been to Church?" *"Sunday School Gran,"* said the child quite emphatically! And then she went on, "I said a prayer to God and asked him to keep Daddy safe from harm and danger." (Her dad, at the time, was serving in the Royal Australian Navy with the Helicopter Squadron flying regularly from Sydney to Vietnam.) "Then" the six-year old continued, "after my prayer I learned about God and Jesus and his disciples." Gran responded, "Well dear, it was good of you to say a prayer for your daddy and you can be sure that God will take care of him for you, and for your sister Jane, and for your Mummy. Do you *like* going to Church?" Gran concluded. Stamping her little foot hard on the floor and waving her arms in the air the wee one bellowed, **"Gran, didn't you listen to what I said? I go to SUNDAY SCHOOL!** You go to Church when you **KNOW** about God — I go to Sunday School to **LEARN** about God. When I'm bigger I'll go to Church!"

Mrs Tookey concluded her kindly letter assuring me that her grand-daughter had grown up to be a very lovely, caring and Christian young lady of whom she was justly proud. Her learning has obviously paid off!

But I'm sure the young lady in question would be the first to agree that the learning about God never stops, and that she, like all of us, is still learning. In her Sunday School classes of yesteryear she had learned about these twelve very special friends whom Jesus called to help him in the task assigned to him by God his Father. Jesus gave to each of these men the name "DISCIPLE" — a word which when translated literally means,

"LEARNER" — and the learning process concerning Jesus Christ goes on and on and on.

It begins in the Christian home and continues during our early days within Sunday School and then on it goes, right throughout a lifetime of witness and service both inside and outside the Church. I always think that today's disciples should be required to wear "L" plates, both front and back, from the cradle to the grave! There is so much to learn about the one who said, "Learn of me". Discipleship, namely knowing God more and more and learning increasingly about Jesus isn't easy, and indeed, the more we learn the more we come to realise — as did Peter — who was one of the original twelve, that discipleship means *sacrifice* — it means forgetting about ourselves, taking up our cross, and following Jesus wherever he may lead us.

Being a learner about Jesus is a costly business!

Perhaps the words of the hymn paraphrase Jesus' teaching on the matter so succinctly:

> *"Take up thy cross," the Saviour said,*
> *"If thou wouldst my disciple be;*
> *Take up thy cross with willing heart,*
> *And humbly follow after me."*

The lost ashtray

HAS anything in your house ever vanished? Have you ever unbelievably lost something and in the end, after having turned the house upside down looking for it, had to give up?

Well it happened in our manse quite a few years ago now when our son David was a toddler. No — it wasn't David we lost — but he was certainly involved! You see, we had at the time in our music room a glass-topped coffee table upon which normally sat quite a heavy crystal ashtray, and whenever the door of that particular room was open, David, in his baby-walker (a kind of baby chair on wheels) used to make a bee-line for that crystal ashtray — and we had to make a bee-line after him!

We normally always remembered to close the door of the music room, but on one occasion someone had left it ajar, and when I realised that all was too quiet for comfort I immediately made off in that direction! David was there all right, but there was no ashtray, and however much I asked him what he had done with it, he just wasn't for telling me!

I searched the room from top to bottom, but to no avail. I even looked under the settee and under the grand piano, but it just wasn't there. I was beginning to think we had brought a magician into the world — making crystal ashtrays disappear at barely ten months old! Eventually I hunted everywhere in the manse for that ashtray — in the study, in the bedrooms, in cupboards and even in the toilets — because David toddled *everywhere* in that baby-walker!

My wife Margaret was just as puzzled as I was, but at length I had to give up, partly due to frustration, and partly due to the fact that lunch was ready. Before sitting down to have my *own* lunch I lifted the boy David out of his baby-walker and into his high-chair for *his* lunch — and as I did that — what do you think fell out of the seat part of the baby-walker? Yes, you've guessed — one crystal ashtray!

All the time I had been searching high and low, David had been following me around with the ashtray tucked in between his tummy and the baby-walker!

In the Bible we don't read about lost ashtrays of course, but we do read about lost sheep. In the gospel Jesus tells a lovely story about a lost sheep, a parable, in which he talks of a shepherd searching relentlessly for a single sheep that had wandered off. Away back in the Old Testament the great prophet Isaiah had likened men and women to sheep which had gone astray, and Isaiah, like Jesus much later on, assures us that God our heavenly Father is like a shepherd who similarly searches relentlessly for any one of us who may have wandered from his path. The Bible promises that should the Good Shepherd lose even one of his sheep, he will literally "turn the place upside down" until he finds it!

You see, that's the difference between *my* story and Jesus' story. Oh, I know that in the end the ashtray re-appeared — it turned up — but I didn't really find it, because remember I gave up looking for it.

God *never* gives up. He searches high and low for every one of us until he finds us, and until he knows we're safe!

SOME MORE "REFLECTIONS" . . .

MONDAY

A very good evening to you! 1990 is my home city's Year of Culture, but it's also Scottish Road Safety Year. It's always a good thing to emphasise the need for caution on our roads — and of course if you want to learn the theory of road safety then the book to buy and read is this one, The Highway Code.

It's so vital that it's made available in several languages from our tourist offices, and it gives motorists, cyclists and pedestrians alike all the necessary information, together with *warnings* and *guidance* of course. But not least, The Highway Code sets down clearly *the rules of the road.*

There's another Highway Code — it's called the Bible! A user's guide to the road of life — a road we all must take! And like the book of the road the Bible is packed full of vital information we each need if we are to journey through life safely. The Bible issues us with warnings — it flashes the warning signals — like the traffic lights — telling us when to stop, and when to use caution and when to go. The Bible gives us *guidance* and sets us in the right direction — and particularly it leads us towards Jesus Christ.

But not least the Bible gives us *RULES* — God's rules — the Ten Commandments — and in addition it gives us that other rule from Jesus himself . . . . "This is MY commandment — MY rule — that you love one another as I have loved you."

But I want to look at The Highway Code with you over the next few nights to see how it might help us as we travel along life's road . . . . and I hope you might join me!
GOODNIGHT!

TUESDAY

A very good evening to you! In The Highway Code there's a variety of roadsigns, some giving *instructions* — to be obeyed, and some giving *warnings.* The ones which give an instruction, an order, are normally circular — and the ones which give a warning are mostly triangular. But there's one exception — there's one ORDER sign that's triangular . . . and what's more . . . it's upside down! And here it is — *GIVE WAY.*

To give way when approaching a major road, whether in our car or on our bicycle is self-explanatory, but there are other times when we must give way — not just on the road, but in the home maybe, or in the office, or in the church perhaps. On occasion we've got to stop and let someone else have *their* opportunity or *their* say! In other words, we can't always get our *OWN* way.

But to *give way* is often easier said than done — whether at home with our families, or among those with whom we work — and even in the church — giving way isn't our supreme virtue there either at times! So often it's our OWN way we want.

But the Bible, that other Highway Code, can help teach us how to give way, because it gives us a very special order (like the circular road signs) — Jesus called it a commandment — which instructs us to LOVE OUR NEIGHBOUR, meaning CONSIDER OUR NEIGHBOUR, not just ourself . . that's selfish.

And if we can learn the Bible's lesson, no-one will be happier than Jesus himself, who claimed to be not only THE way, but also the truth and the life! GIVE WAY! . . . . . and GOODNIGHT!

WEDNESDAY

A very good evening to you! Here's another road sign for you — a triangular one, which gives a *warning* of course.

This one warns us that the road is going to bend to the right. And of course as we approach the bend we must always, whether on our bike or in our car, slow down and be extra cautious.

How true to life! "Every road through life is a long, long road, filled with joys and sorrows too!" as the old Scottish music-hall song reminds us . . . it isn't always straight — often there are bends to negotiate. In fact sometimes for many people there are double bends, one after the other. We all meet disappointments sooner or later — trouble, illness, sadness, problems . . . all of which could well be described as BENDS.

On the other hand sometimes the road is straight and clear and easy — no bends, no hazards, nothing to trouble us much at all — and we're very thankful for stretches like these. We're very grateful to God our Father.

But you know, if we have invited God to travel with us along life's road — *as he surely does* — we can be sure that he will help us and bless us, both on the straight, care-free stretches, and on the bends!

Remember Jesus' promise — "I AM WITH YOU ALWAYS" — and especially, I'm positively sure, on the *BENDS!*
GOODNIGHT!

THURSDAY

A very good evening to you! A very important circular road sign which gives us an order is this one . . . NO U-TURNS.

When we meet it on our journey it means that under no circumstances must we turn our car round about on that road and go back in the opposite direction . . . we must keep going in the *onward* direction.

But goodness, how often we disobey this order in so many other areas of life! Time after time each one of us makes the proverbial U-TURN. We promise to do something for someone — and we don't . . . we go back on our word and make a U-TURN.

Even in matters relating to the Christian way of life, for those of us who profess it, we do U-TURNS. We make promises to God about coming to church and about giving a proportion of our time and money for the Church's work . . . we promise to say our prayers and to read our Bibles and to care for one another . . . and often, we don't.

Now of course, on our highways up and down the land it is clearly DANGEROUS to do a U-TURN when ordered by the circular road sign *not* to do so! And on the road of life too it's equally dangerous to disregard the order. It's just not right in our lives to make promises to God and then to go back on them.

We must ever move faithfully forward, because when we set out on the Christian way of life — on the road that leads to God — there can *BE* no turning back — no U-TURNS! Rather pressing onwards to the very end of the road . . . where all the love we've been dreaming of will be waiting for us!

GOODNIGHT!

FRIDAY

A very good evening to you! We've been thinking this week about ROADSIGNS and about The Highway Code . . . and of course about the BIBLE. Roadsigns are important but so too are SIGNPOSTS.

I remember once going to fulfil a country preaching engagement — on a pretty wet and windy morning! I came to a junction at which four roads converged. Not knowing the area I checked the SIGNPOST which was right there . . . but it didn't help, because it pointed forwards, ahead, to the small town from which I had just come!

Something was wrong — how could somewhere I had just already been be up ahead? And I hadn't taken any wrong turnings because there weren't any to take! The signpost must be facing the wrong way I thought — and it was. The wind, nearly gale force, had twisted it right round. So there I sat in the car trying to work out the proper position of the arms of the signpost by twisting them around mentally until the road I had just come along had the right town pointing towards it!

Soon afterwards I'm happy to say, I found the country church I was looking for.

As I travelled towards it I couldn't help remembering a similar "signpost" story told by St Paul and recorded in that other Highway Code we call the Bible. "YOU ARE LIVING LETTERS FOR ALL TO KNOW AND READ" Paul wrote. In a way it would seem that people who follow the Christian way are like *signposts* . . . for others to follow . . . and which can lead others to Jesus Christ. HOW VITALLY IMPORTANT IT IS THAT *OUR LIVES* ARE POINTING IN THE RIGHT DIRECTION!

HAPPY TRAVELLING!!!

Leaving your mark

WE have spent many family holidays in the historic city of St Andrews, and this year was no exception as we were fortunate to return for a few weeks. The town has been a popular venue long since. In fact it is said that long before Columbus discovered America or Cook found Australia pilgrims visited this Scottish holy city, and scholars of supreme academic ability attended its university, the oldest in Scotland. Some parts of the present university buildings date back to 1450 but the university today is still at the heart of the town's busy life.

St Andrews is also the "home of golf" of course and the new British Golf Museum has recently been opened just across the road from the famous Royal and Ancient Clubhouse. So golf too now occupies its rightful place within the history of the historic city in the form of the various golfing exhibits of years gone by now on display to the public in the new museum.

But quite apart from its ancient university and its golfing heritage, St Andrews is a place which bears many marks of the past — the Cathedral ruins, the tower of St Rule and not least the Castle standing high on the rugged cliffs.

However the mark which I particularly want to tell you about in St Andrews is one which is just a little less illustrious than any of these! In fact it appears on the pavement just outside the shop which used to be the Co-op in South Street! And it was made quite a few years ago by the wheels of our twin buggy — but it's still there for all to see! In fact every time we pass the spot our twin daughters Gillian and Jennifer (who are now 10) take great delight in pointing it out to us! "Our pram made that mark when we were babies" is the two-fold cry that inevitably goes up as we pass by! You see, the bollards which had been placed around this newly cemented section of pavement had been blown away (St Andrews can be a windy place!) and we inadvertently pushed the twin pram over it. The mark is there to this day, and unless in due course that particular patch of pavement is dug up for repair, it may well be there for all time!

In one way or another, we all leave our mark in places and on people, so it's important that the impressions we each leave behind us are good ones. It would be nice to think that people would remember us for our kindness, our honesty, our integrity, our helpfulness and for our acts of love.

And when we think about love, in the fullest sense of the word, we think of course about Jesus Christ. You know, when Jesus gave up this earthy life *he left his mark too* — for all time and for all people. Again and again Jesus said to his friends, "Follow me." Time after time we read these two words in the gospels. And if we do that — if we walk in his ways and follow in his footsteps, there is no doubt that the marks and the impressions which we will leave behind us will be good ones . . . . because they will be the marks of the Master.

Over the bridge to Skye!

THE long-awaited road link with the Island of Skye is now in the offing! Advertisements inviting companies to tender for the contract to construct the bridge have now been placed, and the target date for its completion is sometime in 1994.

I believe that the bridge will span the stretch of water between Kyle of Lochalsh and Kyleakin, and, like the much smaller stone bridge between the Island of Seil and the mainland, the new Skye bridge will actually span the Atlantic Ocean (at least a part of it!) But as someone has said, somehow "Over the BRIDGE to Skye" just doesn't sound right!

Nevertheless the prospect of the new bridge is being described as the most exciting project in the Highlands of Scotland in modern times. Bridges are vital links between communities, and many bridges of course span waters. They are built of necessity — particularly in these days of soaring costs, no government or authority is going to approve the construction of a bridge unless it's thought to be absolutely necessary.

But there are other necessary bridges which must be built too — bridges in the metaphorical sense — between men and women one to another, and between nations and governments — bridges to span the often troubled waters that separate them. I'm reminded of the classic song of the sixties written by Messrs Simon and Garfunkel and still heard regularly on the radio and on television, "Bridge over troubled water". The lyrics of this popular song stab us wide awake with the truth which religion so urgently endeavours to communicate. Do you remember the opening lines of the song? They run like this:

"When you're weary, feeling small,
When tears are in your eyes,
I will dry them all:
I'm on your side.
When times get rough and friends just can't be found,
Like a bridge over troubled water
I will lay me down."

To be a bridge over deep trouble and need is what Jesus Christ has been for countless men and women through the ages. And this song — which is in fact a love song — is surely an expression of what the Christian spirit ought to be, namely, to be a bridge over the troubled waters of life which threaten and often engulf every one of us. God calls each one of us who profess the Christian faith into the bridge-building business!

"God in Christ has made us agents of reconciliation," as St Paul once put it. And the necessary bridges we build must always be bridges of *love*. But before we even begin to think about building our bridges we must be positively sure of the foundation upon which we intend to construct!

No doubt in the early stages of planning the new bridge "over the sea to Skye" (*that* sounds better!) meticulous attention will be given by the civil engineers involved in the project, particularly to the site which has been proposed. The poor folks of Kyle and Kyleakin will need to be supplied with ear plugs during the early stages! Piledrivers will be throbbing away non-stop no doubt as they thrust deeper and deeper down into the ground on each bank in order to reach the solid rock on which the new bridge will eventually be supported. Unless foundations are sure, no superstructure will be safe for very long.

Jesus once told a simple, yet classic story, about two men who built houses for themselves. The prudent or *wise* man built his on rock and it was able to withstand the wildest of weather, but the *foolish* man just didn't bother to take the time to check the sub-soil — and we know what happened to his new abode! In the words of the children's song — "THE HOUSE ON THE SAND FELL FLAT!"

Foundations are so important, and no more so than in the sphere of human relationships. The bridges of love which Christ commissions us to build must be built on sure foundations, and there is no foundation more sure than Jesus himself!

In the words of the old redemption hymn:

> "On Christ, the solid rock, I stand.
> All other ground is sinking sand."

"Pulling out all the stops"

FOR over forty five years our lovely kirk in Nairn was blessed with the services of its dear organist and friend, James McMorran. A well qualified musician to say the least, Jim's sensitive and uplifting playing was a delight to all who listened to him. He was endowed with many gifts and graces but two talents stood out in particular.

Firstly, his ability to give a good strong positive lead to the choir and congregation in the singing of God's praise Sunday by Sunday, and secondly his uncanny gift of being able to produce from his vast repertoire, and play, during the offering, a melody uniquely relevant to the sermon that had just been preached — without prior warning of the sermon text or topic I may add!

But what made Jim McMorran so remarkable was his lack of sight — he had been totally blind since the age of seven. Despite his handicap however, he gave a lifetime of faithful and devoted service to his kirk and to his Lord, but alas after a long illness dear Jim sadly passed to higher service some months ago. Nevertheless those of us who knew him and loved him are indeed blessed with so many lovely and cherished memories which he left behind — memories of a man and his music.

Also left behind of course was Jim McMorran's vast catalogue of Braille music, which was church music in the main. Naturally the McMorran family were hopeful that another blind organist could benefit from having it, and so the numerous braille books were loaded into the boot of my car and transported to the Church of Scotland headquarters in Edinburgh at the earliest opportunity. Very soon thereafter a short notice regarding the availability of the music was inserted in the Kirk's monthly magazine "Life and Work."

A few weeks later two ladies had just returned from a trip to Leipzig during which they had come into contact with a young German organist who was also blind and who was desperately looking for braille music! In order to publicise this young chap's need, these ladies decided to place a request for any braille music that might be available through the Charlie Chester radio programme — and as it happened a particular minister of the Church of Scotland was listening in! He had just been reading the "Life and Work" article prior to switching on his radio — and yes, you've guessed, contact was quickly established between all the parties concerned, and by courtesy of British Airways and Lufthansa the late James McMorran's collection of braille music was flown out, free of charge, to Leipzig! And what an appropriate destination for a consignment of church music — the city of Leipzig, with its rich heritage of German composers having lived there, and especially the great J.S. Bach, has been referred to as the 'cradle of church music!'

Here is a story of co-operation if ever there was one! It's a story about working together, and of sharing. Paul the apostle speaks about being "workers together" in one of his many letters, and the working together to which Paul refers is that of the early Christians being united in their purpose of sharing with the then known world the message and love of Jesus Christ.

It's often said that music is an international language, for whatever the tongue, music notation is understandable to each and to all throughout the length and breadth of the world. *Love* is an international language too — there are no barriers in love either, and the glorious music of the gospel of love is everlasting and eternal! By working together in harmony and by *co*-operating, each one of us is commissioned by Jesus, the King of Love, to take this glorious gospel music and to sing it, at the tops of our voices, to the whole wide world! In the words of the well-loved mission hymn:

"Sing above the battle's strife, 'Jesus saves!'
By his death and endless life, 'Jesus saves!'
Shout salvation full and free
To every strand that ocean laves,
This our song of victory — 'JESUS SAVES!'"

And as you give thanks to God for those whom you have loved and lost, we in Nairn Old Parish Church give thanks for our dear organist and friend who now — along with all our dear ones called home — sings the victorious praise of the Lord of Love in glory!

"A piece for the birds!"

OUR flight to the U.S.A. last summer took us from Glasgow Airport — via Boston — to the John F. Kennedy International Airport on Long Island, New York. We were en route to New Jersey for a summer Pulpit Exchange, and we landed at Boston first of all to clear customs and immigration, before making the short flight down to Kennedy.

The seven hour flight was, on the whole, enjoyable and largely uneventful, with the exception of a little incident at Boston Airport that caused some excitement as we sat there in the passenger lounge waiting for the second short leg of our flight, which, would you believe, had been delayed! A small bird had somehow made its way into the passenger lounge and it couldn't get out again — he too was having trouble with his flight! Every time the poor creature would reach for the sky it knocked itself for six against the huge airport terminal windows, of which the bird of course was quite oblivious.

Our fellow passengers became increasingly sorry for the poor thing and its only consolation was that each time it had to make a forced landing it was fed with all sorts of tit-bits — David and Gillian and Jennifer even displayed their sympathy by each sacrificing a few crumbs from, their first real American hot dog! In the fullness of time however our flight was called and as we made our way to the departure lounge the wee bird was still trying desperately to make its flight to freedom. "I wish we could take the wee bird with us Daddy so that we could show him the way out" said one of the twins, as we left him there in the terminal building still banging himself against the large panoramic windows.

My daughter's comment reminded me of a similar kind of story which I had heard long since, of a certain man who woke up one morning to discover TWO birds in his home! Somehow they had managed to find their way into his sitting room during the night — possibly via one of the windows which he had left partially open for fresh air. On his discovery he opened ALL the windows fully — and the doors, both front and back, in the hope that the birds would find their way out again, but alas to no avail! He then tried to "shoo" them out, but the poor things became even more panic-stricken and began to flap about furiously! In his utter frustration the man thought to himself — "they can't understand that I'm trying to help them — but if I could just become one of them I could SHOW them the way out!"

You know, that's exactly what God did! He became one of us in order to show us the way out — the way out to freedom, and to fulfilment, and of course to faith. St John in his gospel put it another way, he said, "The Word became flesh and dwelt among us." God became human! In the person of Jesus, God came into our world to live our life and to die our death in order that he could identify with us, and us with him. From the beginning of time God had been trying in so many ways to tell his people how to free themselves — from doubt, and from fear, and from sin. Not least he had tried to do so through the great prophets whose words are recorded in the Old Testament of the Bible. But because the people wouldn't — and because they COULDN'T — free themselves, God ultimately decided to show them! And he did so by becoming one of them — one of US! Through the life, teaching, example, death and resurrection of Jesus, God has shown each one of us the way by which we may escape from the fears and worries that so often threaten and engulf us.

Jesus himself said, "I AM THE WAY" and by following him, we are each led in the way which surely leads to freedom, to fulfilment, and faith. But more than that, via Jesus, by trying to live as he lived, and by trying to love as he loved — and loves! — we are each enabled to find the way to his heavenly Father, and ours! As the hymn-writer once put it:

"Thou art the way, to thee alone
From sin and death we flee.
And he who would the Father seek
Must seek him, Lord, by thee."

All at Sea!

ONE of the great privileges of the Parish Ministry is being involved in the life of the local schools. In my former charge in Alloa I served as Chaplain to two small primary schools there, and when I came to Nairn I assumed the Chaplaincy of Rosebank Primary — the second largest primary school in Highland Region.

Generally speaking my main involvement is attending and contributing to the weekly assembly, but occasionally I meet with particular classes in their own classrooms, as opposed to the Assembly Hall setting.

Recently I was addressing a class of ten-year-olds on the subject of boats — not entirely inappropriate living on the banks of the beautiful Moray Firth with the most picturesque harbour on our doorstep. I based my talk to the boys and girls very loosely on an article which my late Professor and friend Dr Willie Barclay included in one of his many publications and I centred my thought essentially around four types of boats — the canal barge — the yacht — the rowing boat and the ocean-going liner, attempting to draw parallels between these four crafts and the children themselves.

The *canal barge* — the original type that is — had to be *pulled* if it was ever going to get anywhere — as is the case with many boys and girls! They have to be pulled out of bed in the morning, pulled along to school, pulled in from the garden for their tea, pulled up to the bathroom to wash their hands, pulled from morning 'till night!

Our second boat, the *yacht,* was ideal — so long as the wind was right! If the wind is favourable then the yacht can cruise along quite nicely — quite fast even — but if the wind is against it then the yacht makes very little progress at all. And of course as I pointed out to my class, many boys and girls are like that too. When things go well for them and when they get their own way, then they're all right and everything is fine. But when things are *against* them, and when they *don't* get their own way, then they become grouchy and complaining, and everything is terrible! "Y'ought not to be like the yacht!" I convinced my ten-year-olds, changing in mood like the wind.

Our third boat, the *rowing boat* was fun certainly, but the trouble with the rowing boat is that you don't get very far in it until your arms and back begin to ache! Eventually even the strongest oarsman (or oarswoman!) has to give up, realising that in his own strength he can't really get very far.

And of course we're all a bit like that — none of us get very far on our own strength.

Undoubtedly the *ocean-going liner*, I tried to persuade my class, was the best boat of all, because it was big and strong, cutting right through the storms and the wildest of waves. The liner has an inbuilt strength — a power within itself — in the form of massive mighty engines to drive it on, despite all the obstacles and difficulties it may meet on its journey across the sea.

You can of course see the obvious Biblical moral and parallel I was about to draw when one super-smart young lady in the back row put up her hand and confidently bellowed forth — "But what about the *'Titanic'* Mr Hamilton?"

Talk about being completely sunk!

"Whose we are and whom we serve"

W HEN the Presbytery of Inverness of which I am a member elected me as its Moderator, I regarded it as a singular honour. Every year presbyteries within the Church of Scotland must elect one of its members to act as Moderator. The appointment involves in the main, presiding at the regular meetings of this Court of the Church we call "Presbytery" and also the Moderator is required to represent the Court on various official occasions.

The particular year in which I have been honoured with this office in my own presbytery is a rather special year in that during it we had an official visit from the Moderator of the General Assembly of the Church of Scotland — The General Assembly being the Church's Supreme Court. It was all the more special since the visiting Moderator in office was one of my former professors at Glasgow University, and who is now well known to myself and my family.

In the course of his ten day moderatorial tour of the beautiful Highland Presbytery of Inverness the Moderator of the General Assembly and his wife came to have lunch at Nairn Old Parish Manse with the Moderator of Presbytery and his wife — and what a lovely occasion it was! He arrived resplendent in his moderatorial dress complete with lace and frills, which is actually proper "court dress" and dates back a few hundred years. It took quite a trick with our children — in fact they described it as "cool" and said he looked like a pop singer!

Apart from the ancient and distinctive dress which the Moderator of the Kirk's General Assembly wears, on the index finger of his right hand he also wears the Moderatorial ring, which too is many years old. This ring is handed down from the outgoing moderator to the incoming moderator when he is installed into office at the annual meeting of the General Assembly in Edinburgh. The ring was originally a *seal* which was used to stamp documents, and on the face of the ring you can clearly see the symbol of the Church of Scotland which is the burning bush. In years gone by the ring was actually used to endorse and sanction official Kirk documents, but it is no longer used for this purpose of course. Asked what he used it for today, the present Moderator responded: "It makes quite a good knuckleduster!" Even moderators have a sense of humour!

The Moderatorial ring however is a symbol of the office he is privileged to hold, and those who aspire to the high office of Moderator of the General Assembly of the Church of Scotland wear the ring, I am sure, with humble pride deeply mindful of those great servants of the Kirk who have preceded them in office and whose right hands were similarly graced by the seal of the burning bush — the seal which stands for The Church of Scotland and which is worn proudly by the Church's Moderator for all to see.

When you think about it, each one of us who represents the Church and the Christian faith carries around with us our stamp or "seal of office". God has placed his sacred seal on us all, but we don't wear it on our index fingers — we wear it in our hearts and in our lives for everyone to see! God's seal on and in us is made up of things like kindliness, cheerfulness, willingness, helpfulness, trust and honesty. And if we can display these things in the way in which we live out our God-given lives, others will see immediately — in the words of the motto of the Church of Scotland Woman's Guild — WHOSE WE ARE and WHOM WE SERVE!

As the lovely children's hymn reminds us:

"DO NO SINFUL ACTION, SPEAK NO ANGRY WORD,
YOU BELONG TO JESUS, CHILDREN OF THE LORD."

The East Neuk fishing boats

WE spent a late holiday in St Andrews this year and while there we drove along the coast, as we often do, to the East Neuk of Fife and visited the many picturesque fishing towns. I have happy memories of several childhood holidays spent in and around Anstruther and Pittenweem in particular, and I will always have the proverbial soft spot for the area.

Of course Pittenweem with its fish market by the quayside is the fishing centre of the East Neuk. The harbour there is very beautiful — and on the Sunday afternoon on which we were recently there it was very busy too! It was packed full of fishing boats — the fishing fleet was in port again — in fact there were so many boats in the harbour that day that they were berthed three and even four deep (meaning side by side of course!)

As we walked around the quay we noticed, not a crowd, but a group of people gathered around who were obviously watching something, so being a wee bit nosey we went over to have a look! It was a fisherman they were looking at and he was sitting on the edge of his boat repairing one of his fishing nets. I must say, it was fascinating to watch. His fingers were so nimble and they moved so speedily using a small hand tool, rather like an awl with what looked like a hook on the end of it. And then, as we stood there, something else caught my eye — the *name* of the boat — it was called "GALILEE'. In a flash it all came back to me. The scene in which we found ourselves that Sunday afternoon in Pittenweem was almost a mirror image of the scene recorded in the gospels down by the *SEA* of Galilee concerning Jesus, when he called the fishermen to follow him and to become his disciples . . . and would you believe it, moored there on the other side of the harbour was another fishing boat with that very name, "DISCIPLE"!

Of course fishermen are often very God-fearing, religious-minded men. They are men of great faith, they depend in God and they *trust* in God to bring them back safely to their home port. Despite all the sophisticated weather-forecasting equipment available to them nowadays, they know that conditions can change so rapidly out there on the great North Sea off east Scotland, and so, in the end it is God in whom they must put their trust.

Indeed, because of this the fishermen tend to give their boats biblical names with scriptural connotations. And so, with this in mind, David and Gillian and Jennifer helped me as we went right round the Pittenweem harbour looking for boats with biblical names — it became a bit of a game!

And goodness, we didn't have to look very far! Apart from "GALILEE" and "DISCIPLE" (which dad got!) David spied one called "SAVIOUR" — which is what Jesus is to us all, and then the twins came back with two more, "LAUNCH OUT" and "FOLLOW ME" — both of which Jesus told us to do! David's turn again! He spotted one called "GUIDING LIGHT" — and of course that's what Jesus is — the guiding "Light of the World" in fact.

Our fishing boat game could have gone on for long enough I suppose, but soon it was time to head for home. However just as we turned to make for the car, the final spotting was to be dad's — and it was a real scoop! "PORT of HEAVEN" was the name of the boat . . . and of course that one speaks for itself!

"It's not what you say . . . !"

"It's not what you say — it's the way that you say it" — so the words of a one time popular song remind us! Isn't it amazing how differently things are said from place to place? Every area seems to have its own peculiar sayings.

For example in response to the very simple and common question, "How are you?" in the Nairn area where I now live, the answer might be "Peacholin' oan." In the Banff-Buckie area I'm told that in reply to this question, locals there are likely to answer "Wachlin' awa'" — and I know that in central Scotland, in and around the Stirling-Alloa area, the answer you are very likely to get to "How are you?" is "Doing away".

This reply particularly fascinates me, because I belong to Glasgow (in the words of another song!) and in that fair city, if you ask someone how they are, they will likely reply "Fine thanks," or "Not so badly" — but never "Doing away". You see in the west of Scotland if you say you are "doing away", the phrase is generally used in the context of getting rid of something . . . . "I'm doing away with it."

But of course this works both ways. I'm sure some of the Glasgow sayings must sound strange to those from other parts!

44

Recently John and Moira came to see me at the manse about their forthcoming wedding arrangements. It was quite late when they were leaving and I thought it very unlikely that anyone else would call that night. And so, as the happy couple were making their way down the manse driveway I shouted to them "Cheerio, I'll just put the door on." The bride-to-be turned round in sheer confusion and amazement, possibly expecting me to produce a large screwdriver, some screws and some hinges! You see in Glasgow that expression just means, "I'm shutting up the house for the night".

It's remarkable how sayings and meanings vary from place to place, and it's funny how at times we have difficulty in understanding each other.

But of course the important thing is that we all are able to understand what God, through Jesus, is saying to us. In order to help people understand him Jesus spoke in a special way — in parables. He used the ordinary, familiar things of life in order to tell the people about God and his love for them — seeds, flowers, trees, pearls and sheep. And the stories concerning all these things (and many more) are written in the Bible so that we can read these and understand about God through the parables Jesus used.

We may have difficulty at times in understanding one another because we come from different backgrounds and from different places, but none of us should have any difficulty in understanding Jesus, because he explained what he meant in picture language — and every picture tells a story . . . of God's love.

"Neighbours"

WHAT a lovely surprise when Mrs Betty Jeffrey and her husband arrived at the manse door recently! I hadn't met Mrs Jeffrey before but she introduced herself by presenting me with a letter I had sent a few months previously to her home — in Glenburn, near Melbourne, Australia! Mrs Jeffrey is an avid reader of "The People's Friend" — as are many of her fellow-Australians judging by the number of letters I receive from that fair land following articles I have had published! After reading a particular story earlier in the year, Mrs Jeffrey had written to me to see if I could help her in her search for her late great-grandfather who had been married a long time ago in Nairn. I gave her all the information I could in my reply and I ended the letter by saying that if she ever decided to come to Scotland to research her family tree, she must pop in to the manse at Nairn and say hello — she had taken me at my word and here she was on my doorstep!

What a happy time we had with the Jeffreys that afternoon! They were anxious to say hello to our children too, and on meeting them they duly presented David, Gillian and Jennifer with some real Australian dollar coins! Of course nowadays when we think of Australia we immediately think of the "Neighbours" programme which is screened twice a day on television here, and which is recorded in Melbourne, not very far from where the Jeffrey's small farm is situated. The children had lots of questions for our visitors about "Neighbours" and as the storyline in this country is almost two years behind the Australian storyline, the children were given an update on all the Ramsay Street news — albeit they were sworn to absolute secrecy before the Jeffrey's divulged even a word of the Australian storyline!

In the course of our conversation it emerged that Mr and Mrs Jeffrey were members of the Salvation Army, and in fact they had attended a Salvation Army service in Inverness the previous day. They had remarked on the impressive appearance of Nairn Old Parish Church with its striking high tower, and they were very keen to see the inside of our lovely church building. I was only too happy to take them across to see our beautiful sanctuary, and while we were there Mrs Jeffrey asked me to play something for her on the pipe organ. It occurred to me on the spur of the moment that a hymn well-known and sung within the Salvation Army might be appropriate, and so I pulled out all the stops and struck up "Onward Christian Soldiers!" Mrs Jeffrey just couldn't contain herself! There she was standing in the chancel singing with all her heart — and not a word of the hymn in front of her! In fact she had a very lovely voice and I'm so glad that her husband captured the moment on his video camera.

Before leaving us our visitors revealed that they had recently become involved back home in Central Victorian Gospel Radio — a local Christian radio station covering a fairly extensive broadcast area. Mrs Jeffrey was due to present a programme in two weeks time in which she was to speak about her visit to Bonnie Scotland and about the various people she had met on her travels. She had with her a portable tape recorder and I was delighted when she asked me to play something appropriate on the piano which she could use on her programme. What could be more appropriate I thought than "The Lord's my Shepherd" to the lovely Scottish psalm tune, "Crimond" and so I happily obliged! In addition Mrs Jeffrey asked me to contribute a special message to the Christian listening audience back in Melbourne, and so it seemed to me that I should pick up on the "Neighbours" theme and say a few words along these lines. My message went something like this:

> "Thankyou to Mrs Betty Jeffrey for giving me this opportunity to greet you all from Scotland. Here in Scotland, when we think of Australia, we inevitably think of the television programme "Neighbours" — and it seems to me that, from a christian point of view, the "Neighbours" theme isn't all that inappropriate! We're told in the Bible to *love* our neighbour, and Jesus himself told a lovely story called "The Good Samaritan" in order to illustrate just how *much* we should love our neighbour! We are all neighbours in Jesus Christ, and so we here in Scotland send to our Australian neighbours, warm christian greetings!"

Later on in the evening when the Jeffreys had gone, while thinking about my short contribution to her Christian radio programme, it struck me very forcibly that not only are Christian people the world o'er, "neighbours" — they are even more than that! They are brothers and sisters in the same Church family with one Father, who is none other than an almighty and loving God! As Mrs Jeffrey had been so lustily singing in the empty Scottish kirk earlier on in the day:

> *"Like a mighty army moves the Church of God,*
> *Brothers, we are treading where the saints have trod.*
> *We are not divided, all one body we.*
> *One in hope, in doctrine, one in charity!"*

A right royal encounter!

IN the lovely Highland town and holiday resort of Nairn where I now live and work, we have on our doorstep one of the Church of Scotland's Homes for the Elderly — one of 44 such homes throughout the country, all of which come under the wing of the Church's Board of Social Responsibility.

It's always a joy to visit these homes and it's a particular pleasure on occasion to lead the weekly service which is held there for the residents. In the context of one of these services which I conducted recently, I was talking to the old folks about the terrible years of the second world war.

I reminded them of a true story I heard of the late King, King George VI, visiting Clydebank on Clydeside following the devastation it suffered at the time of the blitz. I told them of a certain Mrs Annie McLeod who lived in one of the tenements which had remarkably escaped the German bombing. While Annie was working away there in her wee house she happened to notice from her tenement window three gentlemen in long black coats and bowler hats walking among the rubble and talking to the workmen. She *thought* she recognised one of the men, but she couldn't exactly remember where she had seen him before.

A few minutes later there was a quiet knock at the door of her flat, and when she opened it who was standing there before her very eyes but the King himself! He smiled very graciously, raised his hat and in a soft voice politely asked, "Can the King come in?"

I had led up to my wartime story in the local Old Folks' Home by asking the residents if any of them had ever met the *Queen,* and albeit many of the elderly folks had seen her in the flesh, it seemed that none of them had actually met her. However, after the service was over I waited on to have a wee chat with the residents and staff, and especially those who were members of my own congregation.

Chrissie, the most dear and unpretentious elderly soul imaginable called me over. "Mr Hamilton, I've got a confession to make — I *DID* meet the Queen!" "Is that so Chrissie — tell me about it," I encouraged her. Slowly but surely I managed to prize the story out of her. Several years ago Chrissie had met the wife of the gracious gentleman in the black coat and bowler hat who had visited Clydebank after the bombs had fallen. And what's more, Chrissie met the Queen (now our beloved Queen Mother of course) at Buckingham Palace when she went down there to receive her M.B.E. for the many years of faithful service which she had given to the Civil Service!

There's a lovely passage in the Sermon on the Mount recorded in St Matthew's gospel, two of the verses of which have become cliché's down through the years. The first cliché talks about "letting your light shine" — and of course in terms of the Christian faith it is vitally necessary so to do!

The other cliché talks about "hiding your light under a bushel" — but you know, on occasion, there can be something very lovely about doing just that!

We all count

SUNDAY, April 21st, 1991 is national census day and a force of 14,000 people throughout the length and breadth of the country have been mustered to handle the administration involved. For the majority of households I imagine the matter will be fairly manageable. The form is delivered by the Census Official, completed by the head of the household, and collected as soon as possible after the day of the count.

It would all seem to be straightforward enough, although I recall a story I heard — at the time of the last census ten years ago — of a dear old lady in Glasgow. She opened her door and there stood the official armed with her census form. "Hello, I'm your census enumerator," he politely said. "Well son," said the dear old soul, "you'll need tae sell it tae someone else — a've nae use for one o' these!"

Generally speaking however most folks can cope with it, although we're told that this year's census will be the largest paper exercise ever carried out throughout Great Britain! And we're told further that after the count, it will take two or three years to gather all the information together! The statistics recorded on the forms are both necessary and invaluable for all sorts of reasons and to all sorts of government bodies — for administration purposes, for research purposes and for planning purposes — the planning of finance, of housing, of roads, of schools and of hospitals etc.

But basically I suppose, a census is a COUNT, in order to know the number of people there are in Great Britain and Northern Ireland and where they each live. It would seem that we are each *IMPORTANT* as far as our country is concerned. At the time of the 1981 census it was put this way: "WE'RE ALL GOING TO BE COUNTED BECAUSE WE ALL COUNT".

We all count as far as the Church is concerned too — in fact The Church of Scotland takes a census, not every ten years, but every year! At the end of each calendar year, each congregation must make its annual return to the Church Offices on a kind of Census Form on which must be entered the number of babies baptised every year, the number of infants on the Cradle Roll, the number of children in the Sunday School, the number of elders helping the Minister with the pastoral oversight of the congregation and parish, and not least the number of members on the roll. Each and all of us connected to the Church must be accounted for because the Church regards each and all of us as important and insists that we all count.

But not only does the Church think that we all count — Jesus Christ *ASSURES* us that we all count — whether we're within the fold of his Church or whether we are not! To convince us of our importance to him he once told a lovely story about a shepherd who had lost one of his many sheep . . . and of how that shepherd searched high and low, over field, valley and mountain until that lost sheep was found and accounted for again. And through this lovely story Jesus is saying to each of us: "That's how important you are to God — he will literally turn the place upside down until he finds you, until he sees that you are accounted for and safely returned to the security of his sheepfold!

The NATION takes its census — the CHURCH takes its census — and not least GOD takes *his* census, because as far as he is concerned, beyond all shadow of doubt *WE ALL COUNT!*

P.S. Good luck with your Census Form!

"Out of the mouths of babes and sucklings!"

ON a recent trip to Buckinghamshire to visit the branch of the family who have now made that lovely part of the country their home, my sister-in-law was telling us of a children's conversation she had recently overheard.

Just before she and her family were due to come north for Christmas at the end of last year, she couldn't avoid hearing her young son Neil tell his pals about his forthcoming visit to see his cousins at Nairn. "And you know," he went on, "my uncle Ian's the prime minister!" (a major exaggeration, dare I say!) Out of the mouths of babes and sucklings!

And then not so long ago here in Nairn Old I had the pleasure and privilege of baptising eight babies at a Sunday morning service. Of course all the families and friends associated with the christening parties were there in the congregation among whom was a wee boy who I suspect had never been in church before. Later on in the day he was apparently recounting his visit to the church in Nairn for the christening his baby cousin. "It was a huge building" he said, "with hundreds and hundreds of people in it (no exaggeration this time I'm happy to say!) and then GOD came in. He was wearing a black cloak, and he had fair hair and glasses!" Of course the organist wears a black cloak and glasses too — but I rather suspect that the little one was referring to yours truly — another major exaggeration, to say the *very* least! Out of the mouths of babes and sucklings!

Sometimes children in all innocence, get it wrong — and in so doing cause endless hilarity. But sometimes children get it *right*. On occasions THEY grasp something in a way in which their seniors cannot — and this is exactly what Jesus was referring to when he quoted these words of the Psalmist to the chief priests and scribes there in the Temple at Jerusalem.

The children there had seen with their own eyes the wonderful things which Jesus had just done. They had seen him give the traders and the money-changers their marching orders; they had seen Jesus enable the blind to see and the lame to walk again — and they just couldn't contain themselves! "Hosanna to the Son of David!" they bellowed at the tops of their voices. The leaders looking on were not surprisingly angry. "Do you hear what they are saying?" they furiously responded. To which Jesus calmly replied: "Yes I do — but have you not heard what the psalmist wrote so long ago? Out of the mouths of babes and sucklings you have the perfect praise!" The children had got it right — spot on! They had recognised who Jesus really was, and they just couldn't contain their joy and gladness!

Sometimes there are truths which only the simple-hearted are able to discover, and often the insight of a child can be an invaluable thing. I remember reading somewhere the tale of a great sculptor who had just carved out a statue of Jesus Christ. Seeking some reaction to his finished work he asked a young child to come in and look it over. "Who do you think that is?" the sculptor asked the child. "He looks like a great man sir," the child replied. The sculptor knew he had failed, and so he abandoned his first attempt altogether and started all over again. On completion of his second effort he called the same child back again to have another look and repeated his initial question, "Who do you think that is?" to which the child this time unhesitatingly responded, "That is Jesus who told his disciples to let the children come to him!" The sculptor knew immediately that his second attempt had been successful — the child had got it right!

As Jesus Christ also said, so succinctly and so significantly: "Truly I say to you — whoever does not receive the Kingdom of Heaven like a child, shall not enter it."

The great paper chase!

PRODUCTION of last month's parish magazine didn't run quite as smoothly as usual. The firm which had previously and so reliably supplied our paper requirements over the years suddenly went into the hands of the receiver alas, and as a result we were left — a week before the magazine was due to be printed and distributed — without adequate paper!

Anne Harris, the Church Secretary, thereupon made countless telephone calls in search of the particular brand of paper we needed — the type which was best suited to our make of duplicating machine. Eventually a supplier was found in Glasgow and arrangements were duly made to have the paper despatched forthwith. "Your order will be up there in Nairn tomorrow," Anne was assured by Rebecca, a most helpful and friendly sales lass at the Glasgow end of the line.

Tomorrow arrived — but you've guessed — the paper didn't — nor did it come the next day. Anne thought that she had better make enquiries to ensure that the order had in fact left Glasgow. "Yes" Rebecca re-assured her, "it went out on Monday afternoon," which was the day on which the order had been telephoned in. "It's probably a delay with the carrier, but if it doesn't arrive tomorrow let me know and I'll take it up with them," promised Rebecca. "It had better come tomorrow!" responded Anne, who was now beginning to panic just a bit, knowing that she had barely two mornings left in which to run off a particularly full edition of the church magazine.

By lunchtime the following day it still hadn't arrived and so without further delay the secretary went right down the line again to Rebecca in Glasgow. On checking the matter out it was discovered that the paper supply for Nairn had been wrongly labelled in the despatch office. It had certainly gone out on the Monday afternoon all right, but it had gone to the wrong place — to Truro, in Cornwall!

Instead of coming to the north east of Scotland, it had gone to the south west of England — about 570 miles in the opposite direction! The great paper chase was on . . . but I'm happy to say that with almost unbelievable speed our lost paper for the church magazine arrived in Nairn first thing the next morning — just in time for Anne to go to press!

In the Bible we often read of things, and of people, gone lost. A sheep for example — and of course a certain prodigal or lost son immediately springs to mind. Jesus told stories about these going missing. It's worth pointing out however that in the new testament sense, "lost" doesn't always mean "doomed" or "damned" — often it means quite literally "in the wrong place". Something is lost when it's out of it's own place and in the *wrong* place — like our magazine paper!

I'm sure you have had the same experience at home when you discover that you have lost something. You haven't really lost it in the sense of losing it for ever, it's just that it has been put in the wrong place. And when the thing is *found* again, it is of course put back into the place it ought to occupy.

The same is true of people — a person is "lost" when he or she has wandered away from God, like the sheep Jesus talked about in his lovely parable. But when the one who is lost takes his or her rightful place once more within the family of God the Father, loving and serving and obeying Jesus — then that person is *found* again.

The lovely and familiar old mission hymn sums it up for us so nicely:

"I was lost but Jesus found me,
Found the sheep that went astray.
Raised me up and gently led me
Back into the narrow way."

The emptiness of Easter

WHILE preparing for my seasonal services around Easter, I was rummaging through my treasure trove of visual aids which I have accumulated over the years and which I store in my study cupboard, when I came across a huge cardboard Easter Egg.

I've used it several times in the past when speaking to the boys and girls in school or in the church at Easter time. It always takes a trick — it looks so real and is gaily decorated with coloured paper and ribbon. But however mouth-watering it may look, it is of course quite hollow inside!

As I lifted the cardboard egg out of the box I was reminded of a story I had heard where a particular Sunday School had, on the Sunday prior to a previous Easter, handed out a similar kind of egg to each of the boys and girls. The idea was that they should fill their cardboard egg with something to symbolise the season and bring it back to the Church on Easter Day when the Minister would reveal all!

The great day arrived and the poor Minister was inundated with cardboard eggs filled with all sorts of peculiarities which were reminiscent of the Springtime/Easter season. The head of a daffodil for example, a small chocolate cream-filled egg, a miniature Easter bunny, a real live butterfly . . . . and worse still, a real live newly-born chicken!

When the poor Minister regained his composure, as the Beadle chased the chicken around the chancel and as the butterfly headed off in the direction of the church flowers, the minister proceeded to open the last two eggs. The penultimate one had a *stone* inside it, which, you must admit, was a clever suggestion on the part of the child concerned — in order to call to mind the stone which rolled away from the entrance to the tomb into which the body of the crucified Jesus had been placed.

But the last cardboard egg handed to the Minister at the Easter service by one of the little girls in the congregation was best of all! When he opened it he found it to be *empty!* The children in the church started to laugh at this until the Minister reminded them that the tomb into which Jesus had been placed was empty too. "In a very real way boys and girls Jane's egg is the most symbolic of all," explained the Minister, "because it speaks to us of the empty tomb!"

The special week prior to Easter, which is called Holy Week, we remember with sadness and with shame, as we recall the pains and suffering Jesus had to bear after he entered Jerusalem for the last time on that very first Palm Sunday. But let us remember also that at the end of Holy Week there is — not an empty egg — but an *empty tomb*, because Jesus, who was crucified, dead and buried, rose from the dead and is alive for evermore!

In a sense you see, *emptiness* is what Easter is all about — an empty cross and an empty tomb!

> *"There is a green hill far away,*
> *Outside a city wall.*
> *Where the dear Lord was crucified,*
> *Who died to save us all."*

Yes, that's true . . . Jesus did die . . . but as little Jane's egg so very cogently reminds us . . . *beyond* Jesus' shame and suffering and death — *THERE IS AN EMPTY TOMB!*

Thanks be to God!

"If at first you don't succeed"

I F at first you don't succeed, try, try, try again — so the saying goes! A few months ago I had the privilege of presenting a nightly religious slot on Grampian Television, and I am happy to say that when the programmes were recently transmitted they seemed fairly well received.

I chose to do the five short programmes sitting at a piano, and on each evening I played a popular song followed by a few thoughts on the song's title. All credit to the studio crew who took great pains to ensure that each "take" was up to the required standard. In fact four out of the five programmes went through without the proverbial hitch, but one of them was smitten with a fair dose of the gremlins!

It didn't quite come off the first time as had the others, and in the end quite a few "takes" were necessary — the majority of them for technical reasons I should point out! The irony of the situation was however that the particular song in question was the popular ballad of yesteryear, "Let me try again!" It became increasingly difficult to keep a straight face as the floor manager bellowed across the studio, "Let me try again — take six!"

Of course the important thing is that people are given the *opportunity* to try again, and goodness, we all need that opportunity given us. After all we're only human and each one of us falls short in one way or another from time to time. Giving each other a second chance is in part what the gospel of Jesus Christ is all about, and the Bible teaches us that, not only must we give one another the opportunity to try again, but that God our Father graciously treats each one of us in the same loving and forgiving way.

I'm sure you will remember the lovely story Jesus once told about a certain father who had two sons, one of whom took his share of the family estate, left home and lived it up — to say the least! In the fullness of time however his money ran out and in a situation of utter poverty and depression, realising his stupidity, he decided to head for home. "What kind of reception is awaiting me up ahead?" This question must have been uppermost in his mind as he rather apprehensively no doubt trudged along the dusty road that led back to the family farm. He couldn't be sure, but at least he might be able to persuade his father to give him a job as a hired servant.

But the boy needn't have worried! What a reception! The best robe, the ring for his finger, the shoes for his feet, the killing of the fatted calf, and not least, the feast! "Let me try again" in the words of the song — goodness, the son didn't even need to pose the plea!

We have come to know that familiar story as the Prodigal (or "lost") son, but really, when you think about it, the story's hero is quite clearly the *father*. And Jesus' purpose in telling it originally is to show and to assure each one of us of the depth of God our heavenly Father's forgiving love.

Albeit our failures and shortcomings of the past may cause us to feel a sense of regret and of remorse, they needn't haunt us, because as in the story of the prodigal Son, God our heavenly Father has given us — and gives us, every new day — the opportunity to *TRY AGAIN!*

This very idea is conveyed in a poem of anonymous origin which is often quoted by the late Professor William Barclay. In fact it's more than a poem — it's a *prayer*. May it be yours.

> *"Lord bless the folk that somehow never got there,*
> *The people who intended something fine;*
> *The folk who might have lived a little nobler,*
> *The men who somehow always **failed** to shine*
> *The people who have tried to give their utmost,*
> *And yet who seemed to **keep it** all the more,*
> *The ones who haven't made their name at business*
> *Who should be rich, yet always will be poor;*
> *The folk who aren't as clever as they might be,*
> *Who aren't as good and feel their efforts vain,*
> *Lord bless all these, and Lord,*
> ***BLESS ME AMONG THEM***
> *And give us all the heart to **TRY AGAIN!**"*

Cleopatra's Needle

MY wife and I spent a couple of days in the capital city recently to celebrate a rather special wedding anniversary and on the two evenings we were going to be in London town we had booked for two particular venues — the first was Margaret's choice and the second was mine!

On the Tuesday evening we went along to her Majesty's Theatre in the West End to see "The Phantom of the Opera" — and what a show! The whole production was just magnificent, the props, the costumes, the special effects (they were magic) and not least the music and the singing. It's little wonder that the show is still a sell-out for months to come — never have I enjoyed a theatre production so much.

Wednesday evening was my choice and we went along to the Royal Albert Hall to the Proms, and again, what a thrilling experience! The famous circular concert hall wasn't as packed out as it is on the Last Night of the Proms, but still there were thousands of music lovers there to share in a delightful performance given by the BBC Symphony Orchestra. Just to actually be there in the Royal Albert was a thrill in itself. I'm sure it's the largest and grandest hall I've ever been in!

During the two days we had in the city we took the chance of seeing some of the famous sights — Buckingham Palace, the Tower of London, St Paul's Cathedral, Westminster Abbey, the Houses of Parliament, 10 Downing Street (now a more major tourist attraction than ever!) Piccadilly Circus, Trafalgar Square and Berkeley Square (although we didn't see or hear any nightingales!) I'm sure many of you have visited these places too and I expect many of you have taken the almost mandatory sail down the Thames, as we did!

One monument that was pointed out to us in particular as we cruised down the river was Cleopatra's Needle on the Victoria Embankment. It stands nearly 70 feet high, and it first came to London and was erected there in 1878 having been presented to the British government earlier (in 1819) by Mohemet Ali (not the boxer!) And did you know that the statue is one of two, which were built at Heliopolis, the Ancient City of Egypt, around 1500 B.C.

The twin statue, which is even higher and much heavier, was erected in Central Park, New York City in 1879. But back to the London version — Cleopatra's Needle. It sits there on the embankment guarded by two sphinxs, also in the form of statues, one on the left and one on the right. But the sphinxs are positioned in such a way that they are looking in *towards* Cleopatra's Needle — in fact they are the wrong way round, wrongly positioned! When the monument was erected there, these two sphinxs were inadvertently fixed facing in the wrong direction — they should have been positioned looking *outwards* (so said our London guide) in order to guard and protect dear old Cleo's Needle and to chase off anything or anyone who might attempt to threaten or attack. In other words Cleopatra's sphinxs are *inward looking* instead of being *outward looking*.

Sometimes this is a fault levelled against us too — in truth we're all a wee bit guilty of being too inward looking from time to time. We can be so taken up with our own concerns and worries that sometimes we tend to forget that there are other folks out there whose problems put some of ours well and truly into the shade! Oh, not that we don't *have* problems, worries and concerns — it's just a case of getting these into perspective.

Perhaps all of us need to be a wee bit more *outward looking* — remember it was Jesus, the Saviour of the world, who once said to his disciples to go *out* into all the world and tell men and women everywhere about him and about his love.

I'm sure that's the direction in which Jesus would wish each of us to face too — and that's the direction in which he would have us go . . . OUTWARDS . . . into all the world to tell his story and to display his love!

"Worth your weight in Gold"

O N a recent trip to the Channel Islands the Hamiltons spent an afternoon visiting the Jersey Gold Centre. It was fascinating to watch the craftsmen and women at work there producing the most beautiful pieces of jewellery from the precious metal in its basic form.

Jewellery has been made out of gold for over 6000 years apparently, and although the staff at the Jersey centre have had long experience in the business, they haven't been at it for just quite so long I'm sure! Nevertheless they will willingly take on commissions and design specific pieces of jewellery according to visitors' requests — and their pockets!

But not only did our visit there prove fascinating, it turned out to be most informative — we learned a lot about gold that day, where it comes from and how it is found. The children were especially interested and they jotted down several facts and figures in their notebooks — for a future school project no doubt!

Among the many things we learned that day about the precious metal was the fact that it is mined 12,000 feet under the ground (more than two miles below!) The main sources of gold today are South Africa which produces around 70%, Russia which yields around 25%, and the remainder comes largely from Canada, the U.S.A. and Australia. And did you know that a gold nugget is a lump of gold weighing a quarter of an ounce or more? Since the earliest of days 90,000 tons of gold have been mined, and this quantity of the metal would form a cube with equal sides of approximately 18 yards long . . . and not a lot of people know that!

Additionally at the Gold Centre however visitors are given the opportunity to have their weight *valued* in gold! In order to do this the visitor has to stand on a weighing machine which is linked to a computer, and after inserting the appropriate coin (all of which went to a worthwhile Jersey charity let me say) a print-out emerged in the form of a certificate authenticating the person's value of his or her weight in gold — based on the current price for 24 carat gold on the London Commodities market no less!

One of our family (whose name I shall not divulge — except to say that it was one of the children!) boldly braved the machine. The relevant "value in gold" figure was duly printed and we were all absolutely astonished to discover that one of the Hamiltons — in gold — was valued at £438,795 . . . and seven pence! One wonders what the value of the heaviest member of the family would have been — but I won't divulge dad's name either!

The visit was fascinating, it was informative and it was all good fun — especially the encounter with the "I PRINT YOUR VALUE IN GOLD" machine! But it certainly set me thinking, because the Bible has a lot to say about gold. In the Old Testament the psalmist reminds us that the laws and judgements of God are to be desired far more than even the finest of gold, and in the New Testament we are reminded in one of the letters that *OUR FAITH IN GOD* is much more precious than all the gold in the world.

But not least in the Bible, Jesus repeatedly assures each one of us in his preaching and teaching — and especially through his many parables — of our *VALUE* to him and to God our heavenly Father. And in order to emphasise just how precious we are, Jesus paid the ultimate price by sacrificing his own life for each and for all on the Cross of Calvary.

Our God-given lives simply cannot be valued in gold or in anything else! We are *priceless* in the sight of God — and surely to one another.

"Communication is the name of the game!"

COMMUNICATION, is the name of the game — but sometimes we're not very good at it! I remember hearing a story about a woman who was up to her eyes in spring cleaning. She decided that her husband should lend a hand and so she shouted him inside and asked if he would take one of the fireside rugs out into the garden and beat it. The woman didn't see her husband for several hours and when he eventually re-appeared she confronted him with the obvious question: "Where on earth have you been?" "Well," he said, "you asked me to take the carpet outside and beat it — and that's exactly what I did!"

The way in which we say things to each other can sometimes lead to misunderstandings. Recently as Moderator of the Presbytery of Inverness,

I had the privilege of conducting a "Kirking of the Council" service in a church in Inverness, the lovely highland capital. As it happened, all during the previous week I had been presenting the nightly religious "Reflections" programme on the local television channel. Following the service in Inverness a dear lady who had obviously been watching these nightly programmes approached me as she left the church. "Mr Hamilton," she said, "thank you so much for the lovely service this morning, and thank you also for your "Reflections" last week on television — you sent me happily to sleep every night!" Now *I* knew what she meant, and *she* knew what she meant, and I'm sure *you* know what she meant! Her sole intention was to be complimentary about the programmes — it was just the way the words came out . . . but we both had a good laugh about it!

Sometimes however confusion in communication between each other can be much more serious and can cause so much harm and hurt. The words we use are so important, because if we use the *wrong* words, or speak them in the *wrong way*, the result can be disastrous. And so often — especially in the heat of the moment — it's the things we *don't* want to say that we say, and it's the things that we *should* have said that remain unsaid. We have all experienced the kind of ill-feeling that can exist within a family, or within a circle of friends, all because of *something someone said* . . . . and perhaps he or she didn't mean it to sound as it was heard. We don't communicate very well with one another at times.

Good communication is so important — and it is especially important in terms of the Christian faith. The Church of Jesus Christ has the most relevant, vital and wonderful words to pass on to the world today! We find them in the Bible and they are words which were written and spoken long ago. in order to communicate the unchanging and everlasting love and forgiveness of God our heavenly Father.

Jesus, who spoke many of these words, was desperately concerned that people should *understand* him, and because of this he spoke in simple, straightforward language. Drawing from the things round about him, and especially from the world of nature, Jesus communicated clearly and effectively to one and all — and the language in which he spoke was always the language of love.

As in all things, here Jesus gives us the perfect example as to how WE must communicate with one another — namely in the LANGUAGE OF LOVE!

MORE "REFLECTIONS" . . .

MONDAY

(Cue Ian at piano . . . . 20 seconds of "Yesterday")

"Yesterday — all my troubles seemed so far away . . . how I *long* for yesterday." What is it about *yesterday* — the good old days — that's so attractive to people?

Perhaps in their longing for yesterday they are drawn away — albeit temporarily — from the responsibilities of *today.*

But of course, while it can be enjoyable to look back on things — and helpful too — first and foremost we must concern ourselves with TODAY and with the opportunities presented NOW — "The best of times is NOW" in the words of another song!

Many of you will recall the great Bible story of Moses leading the Children of Israel out of captivity. At one stage in their journey God, through Moses, urged them ON! 'Tell the Children of Israel to go forward" was God's message.

And that's his message for us today too! Giving thanks for yesterday, and learning from yesterday, we must now go forward — in the strength and in the love of the God who in Jesus Christ is the same YESTERDAY, TODAY and FOREVER!

So much for yesterday . . . I'll see you tomorrow! GOODNIGHT!

(Ian plays a further 30 seconds of "Yesterday")

TUESDAY

(Cue Ian at piano . . . . 18 seconds of "Reviewing the Situation")

Do you remember that catchy, haunting little ditty of Lionel Bart's from the film "Oliver"? It was sung so intriguingly by Fagin, "I'm reviewing the situation."

From time to time all of us take time out to review the situation, and while we must make the most of present opportunities and look to the FUTURE (as we were saying YESTERDAY) . . . we can each profit from the past. So it's important that as we pause to review, we should carry forward with us these things and experiences worth holding on to.

The boys and girls in a Sunday School class were illustrating Bible texts with visual aids they had each brought along with them . . . the obvious things were there — salt and lightbulbs — tins of sardines (fish) and bread . . . but one wee girl really stumped her teacher as she sat licking her lips and clutching a big raspberry lollipop. "Wherever are lollipops mentioned in the Bible Jane?" said her teacher. "First Thessalonians 5 and 21" Jane bellowed — "HOLD FAST THAT WHICH IS GOOD!"

As YOU review the situation, hold fast, hold on to that which is good and carry it forward — it might just come in handy! . . . And as for the rest — that which is not so good? Well we'll talk about that tomorrow! GOODNIGHT!

(Ian plays a further 15 seconds of "Reviewing the situation.")

WEDNESDAY
(Cue Ian at piano . . . 20 seconds of "Let me try again")

"Let me try again" . . . As we were saying YESTERDAY when pausing to REVIEW THE SITUATION, there are some things and experiences that we'd rather forget about! Things we said, or did, or failed to do. On reflection, they're irksome — perhaps they even haunt us. We can't turn over the new page quickly enough . . . yet somehow the offending text is still there stark before our eyes.

But each one of us falls short in one way or another . . . we're only human! Jesus told a story remember about a father who had two sons — one of whom took his share of the family estate, left home and had a ball! But when the money ran out, in a situation of sheer poverty and depression, realising his folly, he decided to make for home.

What kind of reception would he get? He couldn't be sure, but at least his father might give him a job as a hired servant. He needn't have worried however! What a welcome! The best robe, the ring, the shoes, the fatted calf, the feast! Let me try again? The boy didn't even need to pose the plea!

Although the story is called the Prodigal (or "lost") Son — clearly the hero in it is the father. And Jesus' purpose in telling it is to show us the depth of God our Father's forgiving love.

Our past shortcomings needn't haunt us. God in Jesus Christ has given us — and gives us — every new day — the opportunity to TRY AGAIN! GOODNIGHT!

(Ian plays a further 20 seconds of "Let me try again").

THURSDAY
(Cue Ian at piano . . . . 30 seconds of "Memory" from "Cats").

"Memory" from the musical "Cats" by Andrew Lloyd Webber — and what a memorable musical . . . . a west end smash hit — and on Broadway!

Memory is something that most of us are blessed with — and all of us have memories that are precious.

But we can't *live* on memory — we must live in *hope*.

The famous warrior-king Alexander the Great who lived around 350 B.C. (just a wee bit before our time!) was feeling particularly generous one day — he was handing out gifts galore — right, left and centre! To one friend he gave a fortune — to another, a vast area of land — to yet another a high-ranking position in his court. Eventually one of his officials said to him, "Excuse me sir, but if you carry on like this you'll have nothing left for yourself." "Oh yes I will," said Alexander, "for I have kept that which is greatest of all — I have kept my hopes".

"I WILL HOPE CONTINUALLY" it says in the Bible. MEMORY MAY BE PRECIOUS — *HOPE* IS PRICELESS!

GOODNIGHT!

(Ian plays a further 30 seconds of "Memory").

FRIDAY

(Cue Ian at piano . . . . 18 seconds of "One day at a time.")

"One day at a time sweet Jesus — that's all I'm asking from you." The song was written originally to express something of the personal difficulties the writer was going through. But of course like many songs, in time they gain much wider significance. Countless folks have found the sentiments of "One day at a time" helpful to them in *their* particular circumstances . . . those who are heartbroken because a dear one has died . . . those who have encountered deep tragedy in their lives . . . or crippling illness . . . or unbelievable misfortune. "I'm just taking things a day at a time" they'll often say.

The song may be relatively new of course — but there's nothing new under the sun! The *sentiments* of the ballad have been long since expressed. In fact Jesus Christ, nearly 2,000 years ago, said something very similar — he said — "Take no thought for the morrow." . . . meaning don't be anxious, don't worry about tomorrow — live your life ONE DAY AT A TIME.

It's God who gives us each new day with all it's blessings, so in thankfulness to him, whatever your circumstances, live out your life ONE DAY AT A TIME.

It was a good enough motto for Jesus — it's good enough for YOU — AND FOR ME!

GOODNIGHT!

(Ian plays a further 24 seconds of "One day at a time.")

"Gary bears witness"

I want to introduce you to a friend of mine this week — his name is GARY, and Gary is the largest, cuddliest teddy-bear imaginable! He got his name from the great city in Canada called Calgary and he was brought home from there a few years ago (from the famous Calgary Stampede in fact) by a member of my congregation.

The lady who brought Gary over to Nairn is no longer with us alas, she was elderly and she has since died, but her family asked me if I would like to have Gary, thinking that I might be able to use him somewhere within the life of the Church — and especially with the boys and girls. How right the lady's family were — the children in Nairn Old just LOVE Gary . . . and the adult members of the congregation have a soft spot for him too let me assure you!

Gary features at many services in Nairn Old Parish Church and especially at our early morning summer services and at other seasonal services when the boys and girls are off school. You see Gary goes to school too, in fact he goes to a very special boarding school during term, as all the children at Nairn Old know, in a place called BEARSden . . . where else?!

But he comes home at Christmas time and at Easter, and of course he's always there during the summer months! He even has his own special chair down in the chancel, and he sits there as good as gold — he never says a word and he listens very intently to what the Minister has to say! Gary is also a member of the Boys' Brigade you know, and sometimes he has his B.B. uniform on when he's in Church!

Since Gary arrived among us he has made good friends with the boys and girls in Church, because every Sunday, during story-time, one of the boys or girls is invited to come out and take Gary back to the pew and befriend him until the end of the service. Gary is so big that some of the small children can "bearly" carry him!

The story of course is always a "Gary" story, telling something about what the loveable bear has been getting up to during the previous week! But of course Gary's stories are all Bible-based and the boys and girls know that through them they will always learn something about the teaching of Jesus and the love of God.

Gary the bear has become a great friend of the folks of the congregation

Gary

— especially of the children. But he has become a good friend to me also because he helps me in a very real and visible way to communicate something of the love and concern for each one of us of the greatest and most perfect Friend of all!

"Old in years — young at heart!"

I had a very special pastoral visit to make last Thursday — to a dear old lady, Mrs MacGillivray. I know she won't mind me calling her old, because on the day of my visit she was celebrating her 100th birthday!

She may be old in years but there's no doubt that Mrs MacGillivray is young at heart! — when I drew up outside her wee cottage in the Fishertown area of Nairn, there she was out for a walk with her two daughters!

However very soon I was invited in to her fisher house to find that a wee party was in full swing! Her little cottage looked just lovely bedecked in the most beautiful flowers, floral arrangements and cards — there were birthday cards galore — I've never seen so many! And of course Mrs McGillivray had received earlier in the morning that very special Telemessage from Her Majesty the Queen, sending her congratulations and wishing the dear old lady every blessing on her big day!

The local press were there too — a birthday photograph was the order of the day and additionally they wanted to have a chat with the "birthday girl" with a view to putting an article in the following week's paper. I was there to hand over a very special 100th birthday card from the congregation of which she is now the most senior member!

Mrs McGillivray really is the most amazing woman for her age. She goes to bed every night — "not too early, around 10 o'clock," she told me, and she's up bright and early every morning before 8 a.m. She is well able to dress herself and until recently she used to clean out, set and light her coal fire every day! Now she allows her daughter who lives nearby to do this for her.

Her favourite television programmes are of the sporting variety — she enjoys football but especially she loves to watch the horse racing — *NOT* that she's tempted to having the occasional flutter let me hasten to assure you! But she loves to look at the horses because they remind her so much of her early days on the farm. In fact someone had given her a birthday card with a lovely picture on the front of it of a horse pulling a hand-held plough, and how Mrs MacGillivray just *loved* that card!

It was great to see that she was still in such good health for her age, and long may that continue. She can walk of course, she can still read quite well, and her hearing is really very acute. But not least her *memory*

Mrs Jessie MacGillivray, her daughters and her Minister on her 100th birthday.

is just amazing — she was recalling for us from her girlhood days her memories of the men returning to Beauly and marching down the main street there, following the days of the Boer War, which began in 1899 and ended in May 1902! "I still have all my marbles Minister!" she said amusingly. "I never doubted that for a minute Mrs MacGillivray!" I hastened to add! She certainly hasn't lost her sense of humour either!

"You've obviously had a very long, busy but happy life Mrs McGillivray," I said to her just before I left. "Tell me, what's the secret of it all?" In reply the dear old lady said simply this: "I just thank God every night for all he has given me — that's my secret, be THANKFUL." (And how she emphasised that word.)

There's a lesson in that simple, yet profound reply for every one of us — whatever our age. Long ago, even before the time of Mrs MacGillivray (!) the great apostle St Paul once said something very similar: " . . . AND BE YE THANKFUL," meaning, always remember to say thank you, especially to God our heavenly father who has given each one of us so much.

"She wasnae a believer!"

ONE of the sad aspects of a parish minister's day to day life is to be found in his dealings with those who have lost dear ones — and indeed, what a privilege it is at these times of loss and sorrow to be the agent of comfort and consolation.

A few weeks ago I called to visit — let's call him Mr Smith — following the sudden passing of his rather elderly wife, Kate.

They had been together for over 59 years, and in fact they were just weeks short of their diamond wedding. Understandably Alex was heartbroken, as were the whole family who are too numerous to mention here! The couple lived within the bounds of my parish and rightly so Alex claimed me as "their minister" albeit neither of the two were ever known to have been seen inside the parish kirk!

Alex Smith was a couthy soul and clearly he was deeply appreciative of my visit on hearing about his wife's death. We talked at length about the funeral arrangements, where and when the burial would take place, the venue for the service, church or funeral parlour, and what hymn we would sing on the sad occasion a few days ahead.

Towards the end of the visit we had a prayer together, after which I made to take my leave. "Oh by the way Minister" Alex remarked in all seriousness as I moved towards the door, "She wasnae a believer you know." "Are you a believer Alex?" "Too true Minister — I say my prayers every nicht" he tried to assure me. "Well I'm a believer too Alex and as 'your Minister' I'm here nevertheless to commit your wife in the faith which we both profess to eternal life, and to comfort you and your family, and all who are saddened by Kate's passing. Let's concentrate on that aspect of the funeral and we'll leave the other matter to the Almighty," I quietly persuaded him. The soul seemed happier when I left and a few days later all went off without a hitch.

It's curious, that when it comes to the crunch, the Minister is still the one most families turn to for comfort and for consolation — and of course to conduct the funeral services of their loved ones. Those who have had no connection with the Church whatsoever — and yes, even those who are quite openly, if not exactly hostile, but certainly anti-church — they still, at the last, engage the services of ministers to lay their dear ones to rest.

Perhaps, when the tragedies of life hit them and those close to them, it's a matter of "just in case". "Just in case funerals" as someone once called them . . . just in case there is a God . . . just in case there is a life beyond the grave . . . just in case there's a place of eternal rest called heaven . . . just in case all the people who support the Church and follow Jesus are right!

Certainly, we claim that we *are* right, and we do so on the highest authority! And as we come among such families within the parishes of the land in their times of loss and sadness, like the Smiths — and the McKenzies, and the Browns and the Macdonalds — perhaps through the comfort of God which we try to bring, and through the love of God which we try to show, maybe we might just be able to help *persuade* them that we are right and that they too can share in the confidence which, for the most part, we try so hard to demonstrate.

Choosing our Leader

I T had to come sooner or later — and it's now just around the corner! Of course I'm referring to the General Election. The election campaign is now well under way — that is, the *official* election campaign, as many would say that the campaigning has been going on for a year or more! But by now manifestos have been released, rosettes of every hue have been securely pinned to lapels, the war of words is well and truly waging and the 'slanging is in full sling' as the various parties promise the electorate the Kingdom of Heaven!

Party leaders seem to clash continually on issue after issue as they passionately and very plausibly advance their policies — and the poor voters are left more confused then ever! In the end I suppose the matter of an election boils down, in no small measure, to choosing our leader.

The religious analogy — in terms of choosing a leader — would seem all too obvious . . . but is it? Have those of us who call ourselves "Christians" chosen Jesus Christ as our leader? I suppose in a sense we have, but equally in a very real sense, we have not! As we are reminded in the fourth gospel, the *reverse* in fact is the case — "You did *not* choose me, I chose you!" said Jesus.

Undoubtedly there are many election issues at this time on which the political parties have placed varying degrees of emphasis and importance as they vie for our support, but clearly one of the most vital issues of the day is PEACE . . . peace in the world, peace in our hearts and peace in our lives.

The subject is synonymous with the life, message and mission of Jesus Christ. The purpose of him coming in the beginning was peace — he came remember declaring that the world could *never* give the kind of peace that He could offer. His manifesto was peace — from cover to cover, he dedicated his short earthly life to the cause of peace, and he died on a wooden cross as the Prince of Peace.

At this point in history, when east and west are reasoning together so much more positively and so much more openly, at this time when walls have been coming down and when borders have been opening and when so many countries have been so intently engaged in reforming, I am sure that all of us give thanks for the gigantic strides that have been made in the "peace" direction.

But still there are wars, still there are conflicts, still there is so much dis-peace in the world, and in our often dis-United Kingdom. I am therefore positively certain that all of us, regardless of our political (or even of our religious) persuasions, would readily and fervently endorse this heartfelt desire to secure true, lasting peace for all people and for all nations.

Christ our leader, who has chosen *us*, has chosen us to follow him and to support him, and it is only by doing this that his campaign may be vigorously fought and triumphantly won. May we never let him down — may we ever rally to his call and to his cause, for it is only by virtue of such loyal and faithful support that Christ's manifesto will become policy in the world of our time.

In many ways Jesus Christ as a leader is quite unique — not least in the sense that *he* has elected to choose *us!*

But perhaps he's unique in this respect also . . . when our leader promises us the Kingdom of Heaven — he really does mean it!

SOME FINAL "REFLECTIONS" . . .

MONDAY

(Cue Ian at piano . . . . 30 seconds of "I Believe")

Hello again — I thought I'd play for you this time some popular religious songs — it would seem appropriate! Tonight's is "I Believe". Albeit there are those who claim to be atheistic, the majority, when pushed, would admit I think to believing — or to wanting to believe in something or someone.

"Every time I hear a new-born baby cry, or touch a leaf, or see the sky, then I KNOW why I believe!" the song-writer concludes. He's expressing his belief in the almighty and omnipotent God of creation, and the Church believes that this same God came to earth in the person of Jesus. The Church believes further that he *revealed* this omnipotent God to us, through his life and death and resurrection, as a God of love.

This is why believing Christian people are able to state in the words of the creed . . . "I BELIEVE in God the Father Almighty, maker of heaven and earth, and in Jesus Christ his only Son, our Lord!"

You too can share that belief! Goodnight!

(Ian plays a further 19 seconds of "I Believe".)

TUESDAY

(Cue Ian at piano . . . . 28 seconds of "Amazing Grace".)

Hello again — no prizes for guessing the name of that song — its popularity is really quite "amazing" — considering how old the tune is!

Someone once defined grace as follows: "Grace is God giving us what we don't deserve, and not giving us what we do deserve" . . . indeed, how true. The Russian Empress, Catherine the Great once said, "I shall be an autocrat — that's my trade . . . and the good Lord will forgive me — that's his." But it's not as simple as that — we just can't treat the amazing grace of God as lightly as that.

It *costs* us something to be forgiven . . . it costs on our part repentance . . . just as it cost God something in the beginning to forgive us . . . it cost him the cross . . . the Old Rugged Cross . . . but more about that tomorrow!

Goodnight!

(Ian plays a further 25 seconds of "Amazing Grace.")

WEDNESDAY

(Cue Ian at piano . . . . 26 seconds of "The Old Rugged Cross".)

The Old Rugged Cross! A minister once wrote in his book of an exciting and rather different family picnic — in the dark — and down by the wooded banks of a burn! His children loved it and their campsite was sheltered by a fallen tree which formed a cosy windbreak.

"Look Dad," shouted his son, "there's the cross!'" Silhouetted against the starlit sky they could see the dark outline of a cross. Dad went to investigate and found that two tree roots had crossed at right angles and in time they had knit together to form a perfect crucifix.

He cut it down, and today that rough and rugged cross sits on his study desk as a constant reminder of the *other* old rugged cross . . . the one at the roots of the Christian faith — because *it* speaks of *sacrifice* and of *forgiving love.*

May you, in one way or another, also experience the vision of the cross, and when you do — in the words of the song — *cherish* it, *cling* to it, and by God's amazing grace you too will one day have the joy of exchanging it for a crown!

Goodnight!

(Ian plays a further 16 seconds of "The Old Rugged Cross.")

THURSDAY

(Cue Ian at piano . . . . 28 seconds of "If I can help somebody".)

"If I can help somebody as I pass along, then my living will not be in vain" — that's not a bad philosophy! It's neighbourly . . . more than that, it's Christlike. Indeed Jesus told a story to illustrate the "love thy neighbour" philosophy . . . the one about the Good Samaritan who offered a helping hand to an injured Jew lying there at the side of the Jerusalem to Jericho road.

But the second verse of the old song really hits the nail on the head!

"If I can do my duty as a *Christian ought,* if I can spread love's message that the Master taught." You see verse two goes further, and so must we! It's laudable, commendable to offer a helping hand to those in need as we travel along life's road, but to do so in the name of Christ, and to communicate at the same time the Master's message of boundless and forgiving love, is more than commendable by far!

Try it — and I guarantee that *your* living will not be in vain either!

Goodnight!

(Ian plays a further 28 seconds of "If I can help somebody".)

FRIDAY

(Cue Ian at piano . . . 19 seconds of "Love changes everything.")

"Love changes everything!" — the Lloyd-Webber classic . . . and unlike the others I've played for you this week this one *isn't* a religious song — or is it?

It comes from the hit musical "Aspects of Love". Love is patient, love is kind, love rejoices in the truth, love is eternal! That's how St Paul describes the various aspects of love in the bible.

Love changes everything! It's a gift of a text to any preacher of the gospel, but of course its sentiments were expressed long since by Jesus himself in the stories he told . . . like the one about the mugged Jew by the roadside we were speaking about last night. Along came a good Samaritan and love changed everything. Or the other story about a wayward son who left home and disgraced his family, but who found on his return a father running to hug him and to welcome him back — a loving, forgiving father whose attitude so clearly demonstrated that love changes everything!

On the face of it, the song is secular, but for those who have eyes to see there's truly a wealth of religious, *Christian* meaning and teaching behind it!

Goodnight!

(Ian plays a further 27 seconds of "Love changes everything.")

CASSETTE OFFER

IAN HAMILTON PLAYS

PIANO & ORGAN FAVOURITES

PIANO TRACKS
To a wild rose
Theme — *"Love Story"*
My ain folk
Nocturne *(Grieg)*
Forgotten Dreams
A nightingale sang in Berkeley Square
Songs from *"The Sound of Music"*

ORGAN TRACKS
On wings of song
Songs from *"South Pacific"*
Sheep may safely graze
The Music of Andrew Lloyd Webber
Meditation on a Scottish Hymn
Noèl Ecossais

. . . . . AND MANY MORE!

Available by post — send £5.65 *(including p. & p.)* to:

CASSETTE OFFER, 3 MANSE ROAD, NAIRN IV12 4RN

79